LITTLE MEALS

LITTLE MEALS

A Great New Way to Eat and Cook

ROZANNE GOLD

VILLARD BOOKS   NEW YORK   1993

Library of Congress Cataloging-in-Publication Data

Gold, Rozanne
  Little meals : a great new way to eat and cook / Rozanne Gold.
    p. cm.
  Includes index.
   ISBN 0-679-42135-1 (alk. paper)
   1. Suppers. I. Title.
TX738.G65 1993
641.5'3—dc20 92-56813

Manufactured in the United States of America on acid-free paper

9 8 7 6 5 4 3 2

Book design by Georgiana Goodwin

To Joseph Baum,

who gave me the opportunity of a lifetime

To Michael Whiteman,

the love of my life

Acknowledgments

I cherish my family, a constant source of love and encouragement.

I cherish my friends, old and new, who are always there for me.

This book could not have been done without the amazing skills of Linda Jantzen Rohslau, my assistant, who possesses great wisdom and kindness.

Special thanks to dear Jonathan Rose, who led me to Michael Rudell, who led me to John Boswell.

To my parents, Marion and Bill; brother, Leon; and sister-in-law, Gail. And to my stepson, Jeremy.

To my best friends, professional and otherwise: Amy Berkowitz, Steve North, Arthur Schwartz, Dale Glasser Bellisfield, Leslie Revsin, Susy Davidson, Rona Jaffe, Ben and Phyllis Feder, Miles and Lillian Cahn, Florence and Richard Fabricant, Dennis Sweeney, Lois Bloom, Chip Fisher, Sheila Lukins, Robin Zucker, John Sheldon and Judy Rundel, Francesco de'Rogati.

Contents

Contents

Contents

Contents

Contents

Contents

Contents

Contents

Contents

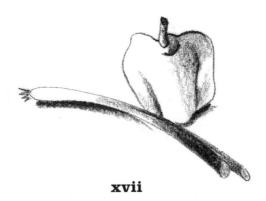

Little Meals

Chapter I

A Short History of Little Meals

From the time I was a child, my daytime fantasies were filled with food and travel. My mother recalls that I wore my first cookbook to tatters, carrying it everywhere like a security blanket. I knew that I wanted to be someone's cook, but what I didn't know was that the desire was in my blood. For only recently did I discover that in 1930 my maternal grandfather and great-grandmother owned a Hungarian restaurant in Astoria, Queens. How thrilling to know I've followed in those ancestral footsteps!

Cooking at home was simple and robust: strong Hungarian flavors from my mother; mammoth steamed lobsters, popovers and blueberry muffins from a quasi-Yankee father whose roots ran from Boston directly to Russia and Poland.

We loved to eat. Perhaps my first hint of Little Meals as a way of life came from my brother, who had no regard for conventionality at mealtimes and ate whatever he wanted whenever he wanted: A tuna sandwich with watermelon was his favorite breakfast.

Some of my fondest memories are Little Meals, although I didn't know what to call them at the time: daily lunches of Gorgonzola cheese, raspberries, crusty bread and Barolo on the roof garden of the Hotel Kraft in Florence; a plate of melting cabbage and noodles with my mother; the comfort of soft-scrambled eggs and croissants in a friend's kitchen; and those Proustian tuna fish breakfasts.

A foodie was born. Although I graduated from Tufts University with honors in psychology and education, my interests were clearly elsewhere. By seventeen I was (illegally) a bartender, and later worked at The Window Shop in Cambridge, Massachusetts, famous for its pastries. I sweated in the kitchens of such stellar New York restaurants as La Colombe d'Or, Hoexter's Market, Café Tartuffo and the revered Le Plaisir.

Life changed in 1977. Ed Koch became New York's mayor, and he needed a chef. I was then cooking for former mayor Robert Wagner and his partners at a prestigious law firm while running my own celebrity catering business called "Catering Artistique," but I dropped it all for Ed and moved into Gracie Mansion, becoming its first official chef at age twenty-three.

From there I moved to Lord & Taylor, as executive chef for their thirty-eight restaurants nationwide and personal chef to the chairman of the board. And then life changed again. Joseph Baum, the legendary restaurateur and consulting genius, asked me to join his company, and Little Meals entered my life in a big way. I helped his consulting company develop concepts, menus and recipes for supermarkets, hotels and restaurants around the world, all culminating in Baum's restoration of the majestic Rainbow Room and its kitchens atop Rockefeller Center. It was there that Little Meals got their name.

Little Meals grew out of an idea about what to serve with drinks at

The Promenade, Rainbow's spectacular viewing bar, and developed into a parade of dishes to have for, or instead of, dinner. People came from all over the world to try this newest of dining classifications called "Cocktails and Little Meals." The ability to orchestrate one's own menu creatively captured the imagination and stomachs of all the diners.

Glamorous Food

Little Meals were always an elegant way to eat. Years ago, when late-night café society flourished, Little Meals were called by another name—supper, a mainstay of the social scene. After theater, fancy fox-trotters sought out places to dance and "sup." Lobster suppers became the vogue, as did "little sandwiches" of caviar, tongue and foie gras. And there was a famous late-hour snack of a "hot bird and a cold bottle"—often, roasted squab and a bottle of champagne. Trends may come and go, but style endures. Little Meals had lots of style!

Today, Little Meals not only fill a niche in our lives but also let us cook and entertain elegantly, often with less effort and less expense.

It's easy to glamorize even the simplest of dishes. Freeze cocktail sauce and serve it as a sorbet to accompany a jumbo shrimp cocktail (see page 138). Bake an ordinary spud, fill it with sour cream and black and red caviars, and you have a "Caviar Dream" potato as the ultimate Little Meal.

Satisfied, Not Satiated

Everybody's doing it! Inventing their own mealtimes to fit their busy lives. No longer do we allow the time of day to dictate how much or what we eat.

My Little Meals break the rigid starch-protein-vegetable matrix by which we traditionally compose dishes, but still offer a charming completeness that makes them bigger than a first course and smaller than a main course: dishes like Curried Ginger Chicken, Poppadum Crisp (see page 16) and New Orleans Shrimp & Chicken Creole, Cornbread Toast (see page 223).

Although my Little Meals are not ethnically specific, other countries have ample precedents for this style of eating. In France, *casse-croûte* is defined as a light meal eaten between lunch and dinner or as a snack. In Greece there's *pitta,* a savory pie that falls into a category between traditional appetizers and the main course. In the Sicilian dialect, *merènda* refers to a midmorning or midafternoon snack. If Spanish *tapas* were served in larger portions and more thoughtfully garnished, they would approach the concept of a Little Meal.

We don't like to sit down in front of huge portions of food anymore and feel so full that all pleasure is lost. Little Meals satisfy us deliciously because they are served in smaller portions. We can really savor the flavor when there is less food on our plates. Little Meals satisfy, not satiate!

How This Book Is Organized

I have created Little Meals that reflect familiar and intense flavors of the world. Since the concept is unconventional, this book is not organized in a conventional way: There are no appetizers, soups or main courses because all the recipes in these categories have been converted into Little Meals.

The book is more properly organized by the way we live today. You'll find Little Meals from the Cold Buffet, Little Romantic Meals, Low-Fat Little Meals, Little Meals with Speed and Ease, Slow-Cooked Little Meals and Little Meals with a Kick. Within each chapter are several desserts to satisfy any sweet tooth.

Included are entertaining tips for little or no money; Little Meal suggestions for morning, noon and night; and a multitude of magical Little Meal menus for entertaining.

Chapter II

Little Meal Pantry

Little Meals can be planned way in advance or made improv-style. Whether you are anticipating the hunger pangs of your family or taking care of surprise guests, both ways are fun. There's hardly a culture that does not embrace the tradition of offering company some edible pleasures.

Depending on the time of day, the range of little-meal hospitality can go from rather simple offerings, such as *mezze* from the Middle East, *tapas* from Spain or *zakuski* from Russia, all served on small plates, to more elaborate or substantial fare requiring forks, knives or spoons.

Of course, where there's food, there's drink. I always prepare for my stepson's arrival with a pitcher of freshly made lemonade, and there's a well-stocked wine cellar for company. Necessity dictates a bottle of chilled fino sherry, a flask of grappa and a never-ending supply of champagne, as there's always something to celebrate.

Serendipity, the mother of all kitchen adventures, can lead you to create the most inventive Little Meals *if* you have your pantry stocked with the basics.

My husband and I like to challenge one another to make great Little Meals out of anything we happen to have at home. One night when the cupboard was truly bare, I made a pasta dish with caramelized onions and herbs, finished with a touch of balsamic vinegar (see page 102). And just the other day, Michael made a splendid curried-rice lunch out of a few old carrots, onion and cauliflower buds. Tossed with medium-grain rice and a multitude of aromatic spices—mustard seed, anise, cumin and coriander—we had an exotic little feast.

By having a large wedge of Parmesan cheese in the refrigerator at all times, you can turn basics into bounty. A simple salad becomes a Little Meal when showered with wafer-thin shards of Parmesan and slices of ripe pear. Slice a raw steak razor-thin and cover with Parmesan curls, a drizzle of olive oil and a squirt of fresh lemon. Be prepared. The urge for a Little Meal can strike at any time!

Arthur Schwartz, beloved friend and author of *What to Cook When You Think There's Nothing in the House to Eat,* includes pasta, eggs, onions, tuna, olive oil and vinegar in his list of pantry staples, and insists he couldn't live without cloves of fresh garlic. I agree wholeheartedly. The following foods should be in the larder so that you can whip up Little Meals.

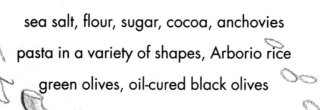

sea salt, flour, sugar, cocoa, anchovies

pasta in a variety of shapes, Arborio rice

green olives, oil-cured black olives

nuts: pecans, walnuts, almonds, pignoli

dried fruit: prunes, raisins, mixed fruit, candied ginger

large chunk of Parmigiano-Reggiano (for chopping, grating, shredding or slicing wafer-thin)

Gorgonzola cheese, wedge of Asiago cheese

bulgur wheat, couscous, cornmeal, long-grain white rice

black beans, canned chick-peas, canned tomatoes

low-sodium chicken broth

low-sodium soy sauce

a variety of vinegars, including balsamic; salsa

sun-dried tomatoes, extra-virgin olive oil, vegetable oil

I generally do not like to freeze anything, but having the following italicized ingredients in my freezer is always a great asset. I also find the few canned products listed to be ready necessities.

jumbo shrimp, skinless and boneless chicken breasts,

frozen tortellini, Boboli, flour tortillas,

excellent-quality baguettes

apricot or raspberry jam

coffee: regular, espresso and decaf

tea: black and mint

seltzer or sparkling water

seasonal fruits and vegetables: eggplant, zucchini, tomatoes, potatoes, baby lettuces, red, green and yellow peppers, fresh jalapeños, artichokes, beets, mangoes, lemons

Herbs on the Windowsill

I'm not much of a gardener, but outside my kitchen window, overlooking my neighbor's trees, flowers and well-manicured gardens, I am the master of a window box. What a pleasure to pick off tiny leaves of fresh thyme, to add sprigs of fresh mint to any dessert or muddle a few for a warm peppermint tea, to crumble fragrant rosemary thistles into a soup or a stew, to julienne large leaves of heavenly basil for a salad. Strong and sweet-smelling lavender is my husband's favorite, which he mixes with goat cheese and spinach and stuffs under the skin of a chicken.

In winter, my sage and rosemary do beautifully on my windowsill indoors.

At a moment's notice, I can enhance the beauty and flavor of any dish I create. I love my window box.

Chapter III

From the Cold Buffet

Once upon a time, the cold buffet referred to hors d'oeuvres *variés* of France, the smörgasbord of Sweden and the antipasto table of Italy. Today it includes colorful, complex salads and platters of roasted vegetables. Mayonnaise has been replaced with vinaigrette and herb-infused oils, and pasta salad has become ubiquitous.

In fact, cold food isn't served cold anymore, but at room temperature to bring out a dish's true flavors. Refrigeration is a great preserver, but overzealous chilling destroys flavor by numbing our tastebuds and inhibiting the very bouquets that make our mouths water.

One benefit of the Little Meals in this chapter is that they can be prepared in advance. Some dishes actually taste better after a night in the fridge, so that flavors mingle and dressings get absorbed. From Curried Ginger Chicken to Pearl Barley & Tuna Niçoise, my recipes capture flavors from the world over, and many use unusual grains or beans, which means you get an extra day or two of life compared to most green salads.

When served alone, each recipe is a complete Little Meal. Three or more together are a splendid way to feed an army of friends, buffet-style. Enhance the occasion with baskets of exotic breads, from poppadums to pumpernickel crisps; from focaccia to crusty peasant loaves.

Curried Ginger Chicken, Poppadum Crisp

4 to 6 little meals

Poppadums from India are like crisp tacos but with a more intriguing flavor, and you use them instead of a spoon. Make this dressing and you'll master the art of fresh, homemade mayonnaise! Serve with little bowls of mango chutney on the side.

1¾ lbs. skinless, boneless chicken breasts, poached and cooled

2 Granny Smith apples, unpeeled, in ⅓-inch cubes

1 red bell pepper, minced

¼ cup black raisins

⅓ cup slivered almonds, toasted

½ cup chopped scallions

Curry Dressing:

1 egg yolk

¼ cup fresh lemon juice

¼ cup Major Grey's chutney

¼ cup curry powder

2 tsp. cumin powder

1¼ cups corn oil

2 tbsp. sour cream

½ tsp. salt

3 tbsp. crystallized ginger, thinly sliced

4 to 6 poppadums, crisped

1. Cut poached chicken breasts into ½-inch chunks. Toss in bowl with apples, red pepper, raisins, almonds and scallions. Set aside.

2. To make dressing, put egg yolk, lemon juice, chutney and spices into food processor. Blend to incorporate ingredients. Add oil slowly until dressing emulsifies. Blend in sour cream and salt.

3. Mix salad ingredients and dressing and chill 1 hour.

4. Divide salad evenly onto 6 plates. Sprinkle ½ tbsp. crystallized ginger on each portion. Insert a poppadum standing up in the center of each salad.

Notes: To poach chicken breasts, put 2 inches of water or chicken broth in pan large enough for chicken breasts to fit in a single layer. Bring to a boil and add chicken. Lower heat and simmer for 10 minutes. Remove from stove, cover and let sit 10 minutes. Remove from liquid and cool.

Poppadums are round, translucent wafers made from lentil and rice flours. They can be fried in oil, but I prefer to crisp them over an open fire. To prepare: Hold each poppadum with tongs over a gas flame. They will brown and curl up in seconds. Turn quickly onto other side. Repeat. You can find poppadums in supermarkets with ethnic-food sections and in specialty-food stores.

Jade Rice with Shrimp & Scallops
4 to 6 little meals

I love entering recipe contests for professional chefs and have been first-prize winner in three of them. A version of this recipe was created for the Rice Council of America. Full of Oriental flavors and fragrances, this dish turns jade-green from an abundance of fresh herbs. Serve with small, puffy rice cakes as a crunchy accompaniment.

1 cup long-grain rice

¾ lb. medium shrimp, peeled

1 lb. bay scallops

1 cup parsley, lightly packed

3 scallions

½ bunch watercress

1 cup diced cucumber, skin and seeds removed

1 large tomato, seeded and diced

1 cup canned sliced water chestnuts, drained

Dressing:

⅓ cup corn oil

Grated rind of 1 lime

¼ cup fresh lime juice

2 tbsp. Oriental sesame oil

1½ tbsp. soy sauce

2 tbsp. fresh minced ginger

2 cloves garlic, pushed through garlic press

½ tsp. salt

½ bunch watercress

Packaged mini rice cakes

1. Cook rice in 2 cups boiling water until all water is absorbed, about 20 minutes. Transfer to medium bowl. Let cool.

2. Cook shrimp in boiling water for 2 minutes. Add scallops and cook 1 minute longer. Drain well and add to rice.

3. Put parsley, scallions and watercress into food processor and process until finely chopped.

4. Combine parsley mixture with rice, shrimp and scallops. Add cucumber, tomato and water chestnuts.

5. Blend ingredients for dressing in a small bowl. Pour over rice mixture and toss well. Chill 1 hour or longer.

6. Divide salad evenly onto 6 plates. Garnish with watercress and serve with rice cakes.

Crab Louis Drambuie

4 little meals

Adding Drambuie to a classic Louis dressing brings a rich and smoky flavor to this dish; you'll want to use this dressing on everything! Use only fresh jumbo lump crabmeat and you'll be creating a four-star Little Meal. Serve with long, thin breadsticks known as grissini.

Louis-Drambuie Dressing:

1 cup mayonnaise

⅓ cup chile sauce

3 tbsp. Drambuie

1 tbsp. fresh lime juice

2 scallions, minced

¼ tsp. Tabasco sauce

1 lb. jumbo lump crabmeat

⅓ cup red pepper, finely chopped

⅓ cup green pepper, finely chopped

2 tbsp. Drambuie

2 tbsp. fresh lime juice

1 large avocado, peeled and cut into 16 slices

1 bunch watercress

2 hard-boiled eggs, yolks and whites sieved separately

2 tbsp. fresh chopped chives

1. Mix dressing ingredients in a small bowl. Chill.

2. In a second bowl mix crab, red pepper, green pepper, Drambuie and lime juice. Reserve.

3. To assemble salad, arrange 4 slices of avocado on each plate to form a circle. Fill each circle with ¼ bunch of watercress. Mound ¼ crab mixture into center. Cover with 2 tbsp. dressing. Top with sieved eggs and chives.

4. Serve with additional dressing in small ramekins on the side.

Pearl Barley & Tuna Niçoise
4 to 6 little meals

Salad Niçoise is famous from Antwerp to Argentina, but no one serves it my way, tossed with barley and a Caesar-like dressing. Barley absorbs the dressing and helps to marry all the flavors. I like it with a basket of warm, soft dinner rolls and a bottle of chilled Bandol rosé wine from Provence.

1 cup pearl barley

1 13-oz. can white tuna in water

½ lb. green beans, blanched and cut into 1-inch pieces

½ small red onion, sliced thin

1 large tomato, cut into thin wedges

⅓ cup black niçoise olives

2 hard-cooked eggs, quartered

Dressing:

5 tbsp. olive oil

2 heaping tbsp. Parmesan cheese

4 anchovies, finely minced

1 tsp. fresh thyme leaves

2 tbsp. fresh lemon juice

1 clove garlic, pushed through garlic press

½ tsp. dry mustard

Freshly ground black pepper

6 lemon wedges

Sprigs of fresh thyme

1. Rinse barley, then cook in 4 cups boiling water for 45 minutes. Drain well, put in bowl.

2. Drain tuna and mix with barley. Add rest of salad ingredients.

3. Mix ingredients for dressing and toss with barley mixture. Chill well.

4. Divide salad evenly onto 4 or 6 plates. Serve each with a lemon wedge and garnish with sprigs of fresh thyme, if desired.

Oriental Shrimp & Radish Salad, Shrimp Chips

4 little meals

As executive chef for Lord & Taylor, I was often asked to invent dishes for famous guests who lunched in our boardroom. I made this for Sophia Loren. I put a heaping tablespoon of red caviar on top of the salad and served it with graceful lacquered chopsticks. You can substitute Japanese pickled ginger and a fork.

¾ lb. large shrimp, peeled and cooked

½ lb. snow peas, blanched

4 oz. radishes, thinly sliced

1 cup sliced water chestnuts

½ cup finely chopped parsley

3 scallions, cut into ½-inch pieces

Dressing:

5 tbsp. olive oil

1 tbsp. Oriental sesame oil

3 tbsp. rice wine vinegar

1 tbsp. fresh minced ginger

1 clove garlic, minced

¼ tsp. salt

¼ cup pickled ginger (see **Note**)

2 cups shrimp chips

½ cup soy sauce

Tabasco sauce to taste

1. Put cooked shrimp, snow peas, radishes, water chestnuts, parsley and scallions in bowl.

2. Mix ingredients for dressing. Pour over salad and toss well. Chill.

3. Divide salad evenly onto 4 plates. Top each with 1 tbsp. pickled ginger and surround with shrimp chips.

4. Serve with little ramekins of soy sauce spiked with a dash of Tabasco sauce.

Note: Shrimp chips are available in supermarkets with Oriental-food sections and in specialty-food stores.

Warm Walnut Hummus, Chilled Vegetable Salad

4 little meals

My biggest thrill as chef for Mayor Koch was cooking for Prime Minister and Aliza Begin during the time of the Camp David peace talks when they stayed with us at Gracie Mansion.

Here's a dish for the latest Middle East peace table—hummus from Israel and *dukkah,* a spice blend, from Egypt. The cold vegetables make a remarkable foil for warm hummus. Follow with little cups of Turkish coffee.

Hummus:

1½ cups cooked chick-peas

¼ cup fresh lemon juice

2 tbsp. water

¼ cup tahini

1 clove garlic

¼ tsp. salt

⅓ cup walnuts, for garnish

Dukkah:

¼ cup sesame seeds

3 tbsp. coriander seeds

3 tbsp. slivered almonds

2 tbsp. cumin seeds

¾ tsp. salt

Large platter of fresh vegetables: sliced cucumbers, cherry tomatoes, radishes, celery with leaves, steamed artichoke leaves, mushrooms, broccoli florets, red and yellow peppers cut into strips

1. In food processor, put all ingredients for hummus except walnuts. Purée until thick and smooth. Place in small saucepan.

2. Put all spices for *dukkah,* except salt, in nonstick skillet. Toast for 5 minutes until spices are golden brown. Grind to a fine powder in spice grinder. Add salt.

3. Warm hummus gently, adding more water if necessary.

4. Spread hummus into a circle on each of 4 plates. With the back of a spoon make an indentation in the center of each and drop in 1½ tbsp. chopped walnuts.

5. Serve with a grand platter of vegetables and small bowls of *dukkah* for dipping alternately with the hummus.

Cashew Chicken & Broccoli, Sesame Dressing

4 to 6 little meals

Tahini, or sesame seed paste, is the condiment of choice in the Middle East. It's drizzled everywhere, on salads and in sandwiches. Here, tahini marries chicken with broccoli in a dressing fortified with cider vinegar, then topped with cashews. Great for a picnic served with a pile of whole wheat pita breads.

1 lb. skinless, boneless chicken breasts, poached (see page 17)

1 head broccoli florets, blanched

10 cherry tomatoes, cut in half

½ cup cashews

⅓ cup oil-cured black olives

Dressing:

⅓ cup tahini

Grated rind of 1 lemon

2 tbsp. fresh lemon juice

1 tbsp. cider vinegar

1 clove garlic, chopped

¼ tsp. salt

¼ cup water (as needed)

4 to 6 pita breads

1. Cut chicken into 2-inch by ½-inch julienne. Put in bowl with broccoli, cherry tomatoes, cashews and olives.

2. To make dressing, process tahini, lemon rind, lemon juice, vinegar, garlic and salt, adding just enough water to make a smooth, thick dressing.

3. Toss dressing with salad. Chill 1 hour.

4. Serve chilled salad mounded high in center of plates. Toast pita breads, cut into quarters and place evenly around the salads.

Salmagundi

4 little meals

This literally means any mixture or medley, but when it comes to cuisine it means a salad of anarchistic proportions, a rather lawless combination of ingredients, all coarsely chopped and highly flavored with anchovies and olive oil. Make one recipe of Pita Bread Salad and add anything you've got in the kitchen. Little cubes of cucumber, cheese, olives, dates or chick-peas make this a Little Meal in itself. That's salmagundi!

1 recipe Pita Bread Salad
(see page 104)

1 cucumber, peeled, seeded and cut into ¼-inch dice

1 zucchini, cut into ¼-inch dice

6 oz. cheese, cut into ¼-inch dice

⅓ cup chopped dates

½ cup oil-cured olives

8 anchovies

3 hard-boiled eggs, quartered

Dressing:

3 tbsp. olive oil

2 tsp. fresh lemon juice

1 clove garlic, pushed through garlic press

1. In large bowl, toss Pita Bread Salad with cucumber, zucchini, cheese, dates and olives.

2. Mound salad evenly onto 4 large plates.

3. Crisscross 2 anchovies on top of each salad. Garnish each plate with 3 egg quarters.

4. In small bowl, whisk together oil, lemon juice and garlic. Drizzle on salads.

Artichoke Antipasto in a Tuscan Bread

6 little meals

The flavors of this lettuceless salad intensify as they marinate in a crusty bread bowl. Cover with the bread hat and wrap tightly for an hour or two. The juices will moisten the bread, enabling you to eat the bowl as well as the salad. If you can't find a large round bread, use a long Italian hero loaf, or just make the filling and eat!

1½ lbs. round peasant bread

6 oz. Genoa salami, sliced thin

4 oz. hard salami, sliced thin

3 oz. pepperoni, sliced thin

6 oz. provolone, sliced thin

1 small zucchini, cut into ¼-inch slices

10 oz. frozen artichoke hearts, thawed

2 tbsp. capers

⅓ cup oil-cured black olives, pitted

½ small red onion, sliced thin

12 cherry tomatoes, cut in half

¼ cup olive oil

2 tbsp. red wine vinegar

1 clove garlic, minced

1. Cut a 1½-inch-thick slice from top of bread and scoop out insides. Save top.

2. Cut meats and cheese into ½-inch-thick strips.

3. Put all ingredients in large bowl and mix well.

4. Stuff salad tightly into bread. Cover with top, and wrap tightly in plastic. Place weight on top and refrigerate 1 to 2 hours.

5. Serve in thick wedges or use bread as a bowl and eat as you go along!

"Mange-tout" Sesame Noodles

4 little meals

Mange-tout (eat the whole thing) is what the French call Oriental snow peas. I've combined them with spicy sesame noodles to make a refreshing room-temperature Little Meal. *Vous mangez tout* (eat it all)*!* Serve with china cups of steaming ginger tea (see opposite) and follow with a plate of fortune cookies and orange wedges.

¾ lb. linguine

Sauce:

1½ tbsp. soy sauce

2 tbsp. toasted sesame oil

1 tbsp. rice wine vinegar

1 tbsp. honey

½ tbsp. toasted sesame seeds

1 inch fresh ginger, chopped

1 scallion, chopped

1 clove garlic, halved

¼ cup peanut butter

¼ tsp. hot sauce or to taste

2 tbsp. water

🖋

½ lb. snow peas, blanched, chilled and julienned

¼ cup chopped scallions

2 tsp. black sesame seeds

1. In large pot of boiling water cook linguine until done. Drain under cool water. Reserve.

2. In food processor mix all ingredients for sesame sauce except water. Process until very smooth and add water to dilute; color will lighten.

3. Mix noodles with sauce. Divide evenly onto 4 plates and top with blanched snow peas, scallions and black sesame seeds. Serve with chopsticks just for fun.

Ginger Tea
4 cups

When you have fresh ginger in the house, why not make your own tea?

2 inches fresh ginger, peeled and   1 qt. water
thinly sliced

1 tart apple, peeled, cored and
thinly sliced

1. Bring all ingredients to a boil. Lower heat and simmer 20 minutes. Strain before serving.

2. Sweeten as desired with sugar or honey.

Baked Goat Cheese with Lima Beans & Bacon

4 little meals

Warm disks of fresh goat cheese crown a garlicky lima bean and bacon salad. Save all the pale-green celery leaves for garnishing the plate. Serve it in November to herald the arrival of Beaujolais Nouveau, or anytime for a bistro-style Little Meal.

8 slices thick-cut bacon, cut into ½-inch pieces

10 oz. cooked baby lima beans, fresh or frozen

⅓ cup finely chopped celery (reserve leaves for garnish)

Dressing:

1 tsp. Dijon mustard

1 tbsp. red wine vinegar

1 garlic clove, minced

5 tbsp. olive or walnut oil

Salt and pepper to taste

8 oz. goat cheese log (Montrachet), cut into eight ½-inch-thick slices

½ cup breadcrumbs (fresh, dried or seasoned)

Celery leaves

1. Preheat oven to 400°.

2. Cook bacon until brown but not crisp. Drain on paper towels.

3. Mix bacon, lima beans and celery in bowl, then refrigerate.

4. In small bowl, put mustard, vinegar and minced garlic. Slowly whisk in oil until dressing thickens slightly. Add salt and pepper to taste.

5. Remove beans from refrigerator and add all but 2 tbsp. dressing. Toss well.

6. Brush goat cheese slices with remaining vinaigrette and dredge in breadcrumbs to cover thoroughly. Put on baking sheet and bake 10 minutes in 400° oven.

7. Divide bean salad evenly onto 4 plates. Top each with 2 pieces of goat cheese. Garnish with celery leaves.

Sweet Pea Tortellini Salad

4 to 6 little meals

It's hard to think of pasta salad as old-fashioned, but it's been part of the culinary lexicon for two decades! You can substitute smoked turkey or even smoked salmon for ham. They all taste delicious tossed with the slightly sweet and tangy mustard dressing flecked with dill. Serve with Pumpernickel Cheese Crisps (see opposite) made famous at the Beverly Wilshire Hotel on Rodeo Drive.

10 oz. cheese tortellini, cooked

6 oz. smoked ham, cut into ¼-inch cubes

⅔ cup peas, blanched

1 medium zucchini, cut into ¼-inch cubes

10 cherry tomatoes, cut in half

¼ cup chopped fresh dill

Mustard Dressing:

¼ cup Dijon mustard

½ tbsp. sugar

2 tbsp. white vinegar

⅓ cup vegetable oil

Salt and pepper to taste

Leaf lettuce or radicchio

1. In large bowl, mix all ingredients for salad.

2. In small bowl, mix mustard, sugar and vinegar and slowly whisk in oil until dressing emulsifies.

3. Add dressing to salad and mix well. Add salt and pepper to taste and refrigerate 1 hour.

4. Place salad on leaf lettuce or surround with small wedges of radicchio.

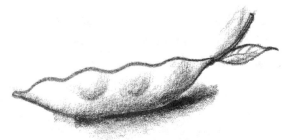

Pumpernickel Cheese Crisps

1 loaf unsliced pumpernickel bread, frozen

1 stick butter

1 large garlic clove, minced

½ cup grated Parmesan cheese

1. Preheat oven to 275°. With sharp knife, slice bread paper thin.

2. Melt butter in saucepan and add garlic and cheese. Mix well.

3. Spread mixture on one side of each slice of bread and place bread on ungreased baking sheet.

4. Bake at 275° for 15 to 20 minutes until the edges start to curl and the bread is crisp. Stores well.

Belgian Chopped Salad, Pickle Dressing
4 little meals

From a country where beer is cheaper than coffee, here comes a Little Meal full of surprises, such as chopped sour pickles and walnuts. You can replace some of the cabbage with fresh chopped endive, which the Belgians call *witloof*. An edible homage to the Belgian painter Magritte—the master of the unexpected.

10 oz. Black Forest ham or smoked ham, cut into ⅓-inch dice

6 oz. Muenster cheese, cut into ⅓-inch dice

4 cups green cabbage, chopped

2 medium potatoes, boiled and diced

1 large red apple, diced

¾ cup chopped walnuts

Dressing:

⅓ cup peanut or vegetable oil

2 tbsp. apple cider vinegar

2 tbsp. fresh parsley, minced

⅓ cup chopped sour pickles

1 tsp. caraway seeds

1 tsp. Dijon mustard

1 tsp. Worcestershire sauce

1 clove garlic, minced

½ tsp. dried tarragon leaves

¼ cup freshly chopped parsley or bacon (optional)

1. In large bowl, mix all ingredients for salad.

2. In small bowl, mix ingredients for dressing with a wire whisk.

3. Gently toss salad with dressing. Refrigerate 1 hour before serving.

4. Garnish with chopped parsley or crumbled bacon, if desired.

5. Serve with ice-cold beer and buttered pumpernickel bread or pretzels.

Chicken Rollmops in Watercress Nests
4 little meals

A rollmop usually refers to a Scandinavian dish of a boned herring fillet rolled around onions and gherkins. These chicken breasts are also rolled, around simple fillings of strong flavors. When chilled and sliced they form colorful pinwheels. Invent some of your own.

4 6-oz. boneless chicken breasts, with skin

4 tsp. olive oil

4 watercress beds

Olive oil and red wine vinegar, as desired

Favorite Fillings
(amounts are for each breast)

Smoked Ham & Herb Chicken:

1 oz. smoked ham, thinly sliced

1-oz. piece of frozen Boursin cheese

Genoa Salami & Sun-Dried Tomato:

½ oz. Genoa salami, thinly sliced

1 oz. Fontina cheese, thinly sliced

1 sun-dried tomato

2 fresh basil leaves

Prosciutto & Mozzarella:

1 oz. sliced prosciutto

1 oz mozzarella, thinly sliced

1 tbsp. finely chopped tomato mixed with 1 tsp. chopped parsley and ¼ clove chopped garlic

1. Lay each chicken breast flat, topped with any of the above mixtures.

2. Roll tightly and brush with oil.

3. Bake in preheated 350° oven for 25 minutes.

4. Serve hot on a bed of watercress sprinkled with oil and vinegar.

5. Serve cold, cut into ¼-inch slices and fanned out on watercress tossed with oil and vinegar. Serve with breadsticks.

Overnight Tabbouleh with Melted Feta Cheese
4 to 6 little meals

This cracked wheat salad is an overnight sensation. Before you go to bed, assemble all ingredients and this dish will make itself. *Opa!* The next day it's waiting to be crowned with molten feta cheese kissed with lemon. The Greeks call it *saganaki* but I call it delicious.

½ lb. bulgur wheat

¼ cup sesame seeds

½ cup finely chopped carrots

½ cup finely chopped celery

¼ cup finely chopped onion

1 tomato, chopped

½ cup finely chopped red pepper

½ cup finely chopped green pepper

1 cup canned tomato juice

½ cup fresh lemon juice

⅓ cup fruity olive oil

1 cup cold water

2 tsp. fresh thyme leaves

¾ tsp. salt

Melting feta:

2 tbsp. oil

½ cup flour

½ lb. feta or kasseri cheese, cut into 8 to 12 rectangles that are 2 by 1 by ½ inch

Fresh thyme sprigs (optional)

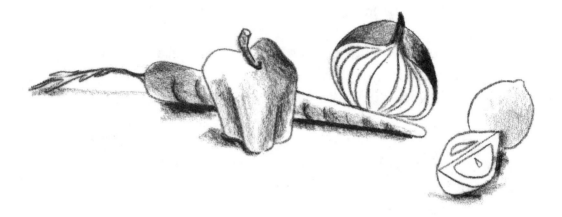

1. In large bowl put all tabbouleh ingredients.

2. Mix well, cover and refrigerate overnight.

3. To serve: Take tabbouleh out of refrigerator and mix well. Divide evenly onto 4 to 6 plates and mound into circles.

4. Heat oil in nonstick skillet. Lightly flour feta cheese rectangles and brown 1 to 2 minutes on each side.

5. Put 2 pieces of feta cheese on top of each portion of tabbouleh.

6. Garnish with fresh thyme sprigs, if desired.

Breadspreads

4 little meals

A jug of wine and thou, however romantic, is an incomplete Little Meal! Adding a bounty of breads and an array of colorful spreads almost completes the picture. Toss a big green salad with fresh herbs and a simple dressing and you will have a Little Meal for two or twenty. Add a wedge of Parmesan cheese and dark, purple grapes and you'll have a banquet.

Breads

Baskets of toasted pita bread, garlic toast, poppadums, Italian bread, lavash, breadsticks, focaccia, bagel chips.

Spreads

Black Olive Paste (see page 59)

Warm Walnut Hummus (see page 26)

Piperade (see page 63)

Eggplant & Sun-Dried Tomato (see opposite)

White Bean & Rosemary (see opposite)

Red Pepper Pesto (see 48)

Eggplant & Sun-Dried Tomato Spread
¾ cup

1 lb. eggplant

2 tbsp. minced sun-dried tomato

½ tbsp. fruity olive oil

1 tsp. fresh lemon juice

¼ tsp. ground cumin

Pinch of salt

Freshly ground black pepper

1. Preheat oven to 400°. Put eggplant on baking sheet and prick with a fork. Bake 1 hour.

2. Cut eggplant in half. Scoop out flesh and mash in bowl with remaining ingredients. Refrigerate.

White Bean & Rosemary Spread
1¼ cups

2 tbsp. olive oil

3 anchovy fillets

1 large clove garlic, chopped

½ tsp. minced fresh rosemary

1 19-oz. can cannellini beans, drained

1 tbsp. fresh lemon juice

Freshly ground black pepper

1. Cook olive oil, anchovies, garlic and rosemary in small saucepan for 2 minutes over low heat. Let cool 15 minutes.

2. Put beans in food processor. With motor running, slowly add oil mixture and purée beans until smooth.

3. Add lemon juice and pepper. Refrigerate.

Red Pepper Pesto
¾ cup

¾ lb. red bell peppers, roasted, peeled and seeded

5 tbsp. grated Parmesan cheese

2 tbsp. sliced almonds

1 clove garlic

1 tsp. tomato paste

¼ tsp. salt

1 tbsp. olive oil

1. Purée all ingredients except oil in food processor until mixture is thick and creamy but not perfectly smooth.

2. With motor running, slowly drizzle in olive oil and process until it is absorbed. Refrigerate.

Blueberry Lemon-Buttermilk Shortcakes
4 to 6 little desserts

Real shortcake is a time-honored American dessert consisting of rich, flaky biscuits bursting with fresh fruit and cream. What makes this version unique is homemade lemon curd folded into whipped cream. If made with strawberries, you don't have to wait until summer.

1 recipe Lemon-Buttermilk Biscuits (see page 56)

1½ cups heavy cream

½ cup lemon curd (see page 157)

3 cups fresh blueberries, washed

1. Make biscuit recipe, cutting out 4 to 6 round or triangular shapes.

2. Whip heavy cream until very thick. Fold in lemon curd. (If you don't have lemon curd, add 3 tbsp. powdered sugar and 1 tsp. vanilla to heavy cream.)

3. Cut biscuits in half. Spoon cream mixture on bottom, cover with blueberries, more cream and biscuit top. Top with 1 spoonful of cream and a few blueberries.

Ultralight Chocolate Cake
6 little desserts

This elegant cake was adapted from my dear friend Edda Servi Machlin, cookbook author and teacher. It is actually a "fallen soufflé," easy and inexpensive to make. I love the hint of fresh orange coming through the moist, dense chocolate. A small glass of velvety Malmsey Madeira is this cake's best friend.

8 egg whites	Grated rind of 1 small orange
½ cup unsweetened cocoa powder	½ cup whole almonds, toasted and finely ground
1 cup sugar	2 tbsp. flour
3 tbsp. vegetable oil	🖋
2 tbsp. cold coffee	2 tbsp. powdered sugar
¼ tsp. vanilla extract	1 cup fresh berries

1. Preheat oven to 350°.

2. Beat 6 egg whites until stiff. Set aside.

3. In medium bowl, combine cocoa with sugar, oil, remaining 2 egg whites, coffee, vanilla and orange rind.

4. Mix ground almonds with flour and add to cocoa mixture. Stir well.

5. Add ⅓ of the beaten egg whites. Mix with rubber spatula. Fold in remainder of egg whites. Pour into an oiled and floured 8½-inch springform.

6. Bake for 25 minutes. (Be careful not to overbake.) Let sit 10 minutes, remove from springform and let cool.

7. Put doily on top of cake. Sprinkle with powdered sugar, then remove doily carefully, leaving lace design. Serve with fresh berries on the side.

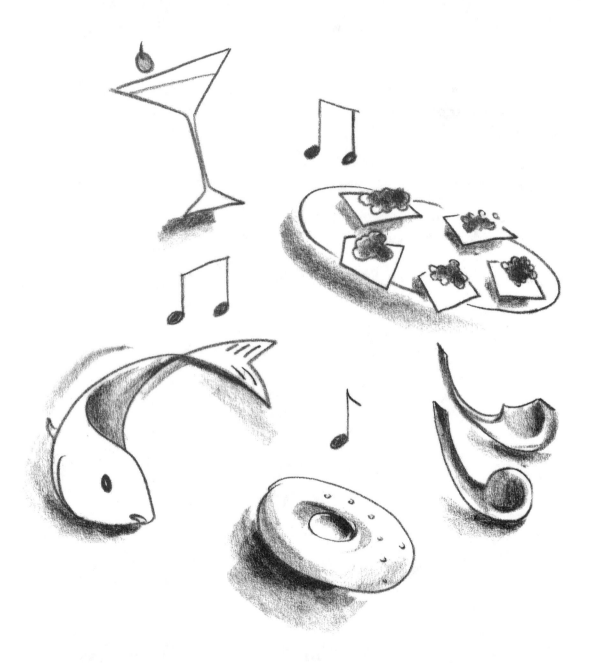

Chapter IV

Little Romantic Meals

Romance. One of its many meanings, according to Webster, is to be fanciful or imaginative in thinking and talking. I say add cooking to the list! Be the director of romance in your kitchen and see where it leads.

No one knows more about romance and the business of pleasure than Joseph Baum, restaurant impresario extraordinaire and creator of the new Rainbow Room. "Dine, Dance, Romance!" is the motto given to this jewel in the sky, shimmering sixty-five floors above Rockefeller Center in the heart of Manhattan. It's the headquarters of the comeback cocktail, Rainbow & Stars, and flaming Baked Alaska. It's also the home of the Little Meal.

The very notion of "food and wine" is romantic; as is dinner for two, breakfast in bed, caviar and champagne, Ginger and Fred.

On December 20, 1987, ours was the first wedding at the renovated Rainbow Room. Instead of a conventional sit-down dinner, we had a serpentine, velveted banquet table laden with … you guessed it, Little Meals to nibble on as one pleased. More than twenty-two dishes, such as tiny lamb chops on cassoulet-flavored beans, and Paris-Brest "bagels" with smoked salmon and fresh goat cheese, created this Little Meal extravaganza. A new tradition of wedding food began.

My selection of romantic Little Meals ranges from the obvious to the clandestine. Cake of Steak Tartare "Iced" with Black Caviar, and Cupid's Meatloaf, complete with heart-shaped croutons and cocktail-onion arrow, make the point quite well. Swordfish Skewered on Rosemary Branches or Japanese Custard in a Whole Red Pepper less so, but they do evoke a mood and feeling.

Sharing a Cherry Tomato Boboli or any dish with smoked salmon says romance to me. Add crystal and candlelight, and any meal can be romantic. An omelet and a glass of champagne? Lights, please.

Crab Dewey Shortcake

4 little meals

Here's a rich dish from a generation ago that's worth reviving. The new twist is shortcake: a heavenly buttermilk biscuit instead of old-fashioned toast points. Good crab is expensive but worth it; less than a pound feeds four royally.

3 tbsp. butter

3 tbsp. chopped shallots

1 cup sliced fresh mushrooms

3 tbsp. chopped red pepper

3 tbsp. chopped green pepper

¾ lb. jumbo lump crabmeat

2 tbsp. brandy

⅓ cup heavy cream

2 tbsp. parsley

Pinch of salt and cayenne pepper

4 freshly made lemon-buttermilk biscuits, 3 inches in diameter (see page 56)

¼ cup chopped parsley

1. Melt butter in medium pan and add shallots, mushrooms and peppers. Sauté until soft but not brown.

2. Add crabmeat and cook 2 minutes. Add brandy and heat 1 minute.

3. Add heavy cream, parsley, salt and cayenne. Cook for 5 minutes until sauce has thickened slightly.

4. Split biscuits in half. Spoon Crab Dewey over bottoms of biscuits and cover with top halves.

5. Sprinkle each with 1 tbsp. chopped parsley.

Lemon-Buttermilk Biscuits
4 to 6 biscuits

1½ cups flour

½ tsp. salt

2 tsp. baking powder

½ tsp. baking soda

1 tsp. sugar

4 tbsp. unsalted butter

Grated rind of 1 lemon

⅔ cup buttermilk

1. Preheat oven to 400°.

2. Sift together dry ingredients.

3. Cut butter into small pieces and incorporate into flour mixture.

4. Add grated lemon rind and buttermilk and mix lightly.

5. Turn dough onto floured board. Roll out to 1-inch thickness. Cut out 3-inch round biscuits.

6. Put on lightly greased baking sheet. Bake 12 to 15 minutes.

Cake of Steak Tartare "Iced" with Black Caviar

4 little meals

My birthday is on New Year's Day and this is absolutely my favorite celebration meal. Champagne wishes and caviar dreams fill my mind when I blow out the candles each year. Use the best kind of caviar and slather on as much as you can afford.

12 oz. fresh ground filet mignon

½ tsp. Worcestershire sauce

¼ tsp. Tabasco sauce

2 tsp. cornichons, finely diced

2 tsp. capers, minced fine

1 tsp. shallots, finely diced

½ tsp. salt

1½ tbsp. Dijon mustard

4 slices round brioche toast, 3¼ inches in diameter, or good-quality bread

4 oz. Sevruga caviar

¼ cup chopped fresh chives

4 lemon halves

1. In mixing bowl combine meat well with all condiments.

2. Make 4 patties that are ½ inch thick and 3¼ inches in diameter. Place on top of brioche toast.

3. Spread 1 oz. caviar evenly on top of each patty.

4. Put "cakes" in center of 4 large plates. Sprinkle chives around the cakes and serve each with a lemon half.

Scallops Provençale on Olive Toast

4 little meals

Close your eyes and think of the south of France. Use small sea scallops on toast rounds and these become marvelous hors d'oeuvres; use extra-large ones and you have a little meal bursting with the flavors of Provence. Start off with a Pousse Rapière (see opposite), a favorite apéritif from that part of the world.

2 tbsp. olive oil

¼ cup finely chopped shallots

2 cloves garlic, minced

1 lb. fresh plum tomatoes, coarsely chopped

1 cup sliced celery, ⅛ inch thick on bias

2 tbsp. dry vermouth

1 tsp. tomato paste

½ tsp. dried tarragon

2 tbsp. heavy cream

1 tbsp. capers, drained

¼ cup minced fresh parsley

¼ tsp. salt

1 lb. sea scallops

½ cup Black Olive Paste
(see opposite) plus 4 tsp. for garnish

8 French bread croutons, ½ inch thick, lightly toasted

1. In large frying pan, heat olive oil, shallots and garlic. Sauté 5 minutes until soft but not brown.

2. Add tomatoes and celery and cook 10 minutes, stirring often.

3. Add vermouth, tomato paste, tarragon, cream, capers, parsley and salt. Cook over high heat 2 minutes.

4. Lower heat, add scallops and cook 3 minutes or only until they lose their translucence.

5. Spread 1 tbsp. olive paste on each of 8 lightly toasted croutons. Put 2 croutons in center of each plate. Divide scallops evenly over olive toasts. Top each with ½ tsp. dollop of olive paste.

Black Olive Paste

¾ cup

1 cup pitted cured black olives

1 tbsp. capers, drained

5 flat anchovies

2 garlic cloves

1 tbsp. fresh lemon juice

5 tbsp. fruity olive oil

1. In food processor, put olives, capers, anchovies, garlic cloves and lemon juice.

2. With motor running, slowly add oil until smooth.

Note: Olive paste can be purchased in a jar in specialty-food stores.

Pousse Rapière

1 drink

Fill glass with ice. Add a shot of Armagnac. Add orange slice and top with dry sparkling white wine or champagne.

Cupid's Meatloaf, Tomato Glaze & Onion Arrows

4 little meals

I thought meatloaf was supposed to be shaped like a heart because that's the way my mother always made it! This is a charming Little Meal, speared with a cocktail-onion arrow and served between heart-shaped croutons. For Valentine's Day, of course, but how about on Monday for the family?

1½ tbsp. butter

1 cup finely chopped onion

1¼ lbs. ground sirloin

¼ cup seasoned breadcrumbs

1 tbsp. Dijon mustard

3 tbsp. catsup

1 clove garlic, put through garlic press

½ tsp. salt

1 egg yolk

2 tbsp. ice water

2 tbsp. catsup to cover top of meat-loaf

🖋

8 crouton "hearts"

4 onion "arrows"

Flat parsley or watercress

1. Preheat oven to 350°.

2. In small pan, heat butter. Add onion and cook until soft and lightly browned. Reserve.

3. In medium bowl, put meat, breadcrumbs, mustard, catsup, garlic, salt and the onions. Blend well.

4. Add egg yolk and ice water. Mix well with hands and form into 4 hearts that are 1 inch high.

5. Put hearts in shallow baking pan. Spoon ½ tbsp. catsup evenly over the top of each heart. Bake for 30 minutes.

6. On each of 4 plates put 1 crouton heart and place meatloaf on top. Cover with second crouton heart. Stick an onion skewer through the side of each meatloaf. Garnish with flat parsley or watercress.

To make "heart" croutons:
8 slices thin white bread

1 tbsp. butter

1. Cut each slice of bread with a 4-inch heart-shaped cookie cutter.

2. Heat butter in small nonstick skillet. Add hearts and lightly brown on each side until firm to the touch.

To make onion "arrows":
16 cocktail onions

4 6-inch skewers

Put 4 onions on each skewer, placing them toward the end of the skewer, leaving room to stick into each meatloaf heart.

61

Poached Eggs Piperade

4 little meals

Piperade is a wonderful tomato compote, often mixed into soft scrambled eggs. If you make a large batch you can have Little Meals for a week. It's also great with sliced steak, grilled salmon or as a canapé with melted cheese. It hails from the Basque country and is a distant cousin of the famed ratatouille of Nice. Pip-pip-erade!

3½ cups Piperade (see opposite), hot

8 large croutons (½-inch-thick slices from French bread)

8 poached eggs

1 cup Hollandaise Sauce (optional) (see opposite)

4 fresh basil sprigs

1. Toast croutons on both sides.

2. Place 2 croutons side by side in 4 individual casserole dishes. Mound with piperade, allowing some to overflow onto casserole.

3. Top with poached eggs (and Hollandaise sauce, if you wish).

4. Garnish with fresh basil.

Piperade

¼ cup vegetable oil

1 fresh jalapeño pepper, minced

½ lb. yellow onions, chopped

1½ lbs. tomatoes, chopped

1 medium red bell pepper, in ¼-inch dice

½ lb. zucchini, in ¼-inch dice

1 tbsp. red wine vinegar

½ tbsp. honey

2 tbsp. basil leaves, minced

1 tsp. salt

⅛ tsp. black pepper

1. Put oil in large pan. Heat, then add minced jalapeño pepper and onions. Sauté 5 minutes.

2. Add remaining ingredients and cook over low heat for 30 minutes, stirring often.

Hollandaise Sauce

3 egg yolks

2 tbsp. fresh lemon juice

1 tsp. freshly grated lemon rind

¼ tsp. salt

⅛ tsp. cayenne

½ cup unsalted butter, melted and hot

1. In food processor, put egg yolks. Blend.

2. Add lemon juice, rind, salt and cayenne. Blend.

3. With motor running, slowly add butter until sauce thickens.

Pan-Seared Foie Gras, Sun-Dried Cranberry Sauce
4 little meals

There are two taste memories that will forever linger in my mind: my first glass of Château d'Yquem (1927, no less!), and my first melting mouthful of sautéed foie gras at restaurant Troisgros in Roanne, France.

You can substitute venison medallions or filet mignon if you can't find fresh foie gras, and this Little Meal will still be cause for celebration. The sauce will make you feel like a three-star chef.

Dried Cranberry Sauce:

½ cup dried cranberries

½ cup hot water

1 tbsp. cognac

2 tsp. sugar

3 tbsp. water

2¼ cups beef broth

3 tbsp. cognac

1½ tbsp. red wine vinegar

½ tsp. black peppercorns, crushed

4 cloves

1 bay leaf

1 tsp. cornstarch dissolved in 1 tsp. water

🍃

1 tbsp. vegetable oil

4 3-oz. slices foie gras or 12 duck livers

🍃

4 slices white toast, crusts removed, or brioche toast

1. In small bowl soak dried cranberries in hot water and cognac for 30 minutes.

2. Prepare sauce in medium enameled saucepan. Heat sugar with water until it caramelizes, about 5 minutes.

3. Add beef broth, cognac, vinegar, peppercorns, cloves and bay leaf. Cook over low heat and reduce to 1 cup. Put through sieve to remove peppercorns, cloves and bay leaf. Return liquid to saucepan.

4. Drain dried cranberries and add to sauce. Heat gently and add dissolved cornstarch. Let thicken slightly.

5. In nonstick skillet heat a small amount of oil. Sear foie gras or duck livers in hot pan on both sides until medium-rare, about 2 to 3 minutes.

6. To serve, put 1 slice toast on each plate. Add foie gras or duck livers and pour sauce on top.

Napoleon of Gorgonzola, Pears & Walnuts
4 little meals

I've always been a little fearful of puff pastry—that rich and delicate dough of a hundred layers. But this awesome Little Meal is a cinch if you use frozen puff pastry found in your supermarket. It goes crackle and pop in your mouth. Sensational with a glass of demi-sec champagne.

½ lb. puff pastry

8 oz. Gorgonzola, at room temperature

3 oz. cream cheese, at room temperature

1 tbsp. grappa or brandy

2 ripe pears, thinly sliced

½ cup walnuts, chopped

½ tbsp. cornstarch

Fresh herbs, watercress or mixed greens for garnish

Walnut oil and champagne vinegar (optional dressing)

1. Preheat oven to 375°.

2. Roll out pastry to an 8- by 8-inch square. Cut in half, put one piece on top of the other and press lightly. Bake for 20 minutes until golden brown. Cool.

3. Mix cheeses and grappa in food processor until very smooth.

4. Cut pastry horizontally into 3 equal parts.

5. Spread half the cheese mixture on bottom puff pastry sheet. Top with thin layer of pears and sprinkle with nuts.

6. Top with second sheet and repeat. Cover with top and press lightly. Refrigerate 20 minutes.

7. Dust with cornstarch through a sieve. Cut into 4 pieces and garnish with herbs, watercress or a small green salad. Dress greens with a drizzle of walnut oil and champagne vinegar, if desired.

Lemon Pasta with Asparagus
4 little meals

This recipe, which I created for the Rainbow Room, was inspired by a friend who is a divine chef and cookbook author. Francesco de' Rogati's home is always filled with opera and great food. This dish is truly *da morire* (to die for!), and even Barnabo, the cat, joined us for dinner.

1 cup white wine

3 tbsp. chopped shallots

Juice of 2 lemons

Grated rind of 2 lemons

1½ cups heavy cream

⅓ cup grated Parmesan cheese

4 tbsp. butter, cut into small pieces

10 blanched asparagus stalks, cut into ½-inch pieces

¾ lb. fresh fettucine, cooked al dente

2 tbsp. grated Parmesan cheese

Salt and cayenne pepper to taste

Zest of 1 lemon

1 tbsp. chives, minced

1 tbsp. basil or mint, minced

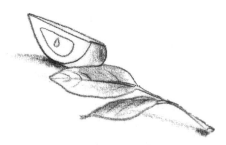

1. Pour white wine into a pan with the shallots. Reduce over moderate heat to one-half and strain. Return to pan.

2. Add lemon juice and rind. Simmer 2 minutes.

3. Add heavy cream. Bring to boil, lower heat and add ⅓ cup cheese. Simmer very slowly, whisking constantly, 3 to 4 minutes or until sauce has thickened. Cut in cold butter and cook 1 minute.

4. Add asparagus, pasta, cheese, salt and a pinch of cayenne. Toss well.

5. Divide evenly into heated soup plates. Sprinkle lemon zest and fresh herbs on top. Serve at once.

St. Tropez Tart

4 little meals

I created this dish for Pour La France, a chain of bakery cafés in Colorado. It is *the* place on Main Street, Aspen, to breakfast, lunch or "après-ski." Sun-dried tomatoes and olives suspended in a light custard are sure to make you think of the beach and St. Tropez. Can be served hot or at room temperature alongside a simple salad.

1 9-inch pie shell, unbaked

4 oz. mozzarella, shredded

2 tbsp. grated Parmesan cheese

½ tsp. dried oregano leaves

½ tsp. dried thyme leaves

2 tbsp. minced onion

1 tbsp. pitted Greek olives, slivered

2 tbsp. sun-dried tomatoes, slivered

1 small zucchini, sliced into thin ⅛-inch rounds

8 tomato slices, patted dry

1 cup half-and-half

2 eggs

1 tbsp. grated Parmesan cheese

1. Preheat oven to 375°.

2. Put unbaked pie shell on baking sheet.

3. In bottom of pie shell, scatter shredded mozzarella. Sprinkle with Parmesan cheese, oregano, thyme, onion, olives and sun-dried tomatoes.

4. Put sliced zucchini rounds slightly overlapping so that they cover the entire quiche.

5. Place tomato slices on top of zucchini to cover quiche.

6. Blend half-and-half and eggs thoroughly and pour gently into pie shell. There will be some left over.

7. Bake for 15 minutes. Pour in remaining custard mixture. Sprinkle with 1 tbsp. Parmesan cheese. Continue baking 20 minutes.

Swordfish Skewered on Rosemary Branches

4 little meals

Sweet red tomatoes, chilled and glistening, form a theatrical back-drop for chunks of swordfish grilled on nature's own skewers—fragrant branches of rosemary. Serve with a dollop of Rosemary Mayonnaise (see opposite) and you'll be asked for an encore.

1 lb. swordfish

8 long, sturdy rosemary branches

2 tbsp. olive oil

Salt and pepper, to taste

Dressing:

¼ cup olive oil

1 tsp. Dijon mustard

1 tsp. Worcestershire sauce

1 tsp. fresh lemon juice

½ tsp. minced fresh rosemary

8 ripe plum tomatoes, thinly sliced

1. Cut swordfish into 40 ¾-inch cubes. Remove most of the leaves from the rosemary branches, leaving 1½ inches of leaves on top.

2. Thread 5 swordfish cubes on each branch. Cover leaves with small pieces of foil to keep them from burning. Place skewers on baking sheet. Brush with oil, cover and refrigerate until ready to use.

3. In small bowl, whisk together ingredients for dressing. Reserve.

4. Place skewers on hot outdoor grill and cook until brown on the outside and juicy in the center. You can also cook the skewers in a nonstick skillet over high heat or broil them. Sprinkle with salt and pepper.

5. Arrange tomatoes on 4 large plates, overlapping to form concentric circles. Place two skewers on top of each tomato salad and drizzle with 1½ tbsp. dressing.

6. Optional: Serve with little ramekins of rosemary mayonnaise.

Rosemary Mayonnaise

½ cup mayonnaise

1 tsp. distilled white vinegar

1 tsp. minced fresh rosemary

Mix all ingredients in bowl. Chill.

Smoked Salmon & Cucumber Linguine
4 little meals

This is what I serve at home when famous chefs and food critics come to dine. There's something ethereal about warm smoked salmon bathed in a light cream sauce tossed with pasta. But the real taste surprise is the cool, green flesh of crunchy diced cucumber. Pop the cork of a rich, buttery chardonnay and serve to your favorite critics.

3 tbsp. olive oil

½ cup finely chopped scallions, white and green parts

½ cup white wine

1 cup heavy cream

3 tbsp. butter

¼ cup Parmesan cheese

⅔ cup diced cucumber, peeled and seeded

⅔ cup frozen peas, defrosted

½ lb. smoked salmon, in ⅛-inch strips

8 cherry tomatoes, cut in half

¾ lb. linguine, cooked

2 tbsp. finely chopped parsley

1. Cook olive oil and scallions in nonstick skillet for 1 minute.

2. Add white wine, cream, butter and half the Parmesan cheese and cook over high heat for 2 minutes until sauce begins to thicken.

3. Add diced cucumber, peas, smoked salmon and cherry tomatoes. Cook over high heat for 1 minute.

4. Add linguine to pan and mix well with sauce.

5. Divide pasta evenly into bowls. Sprinkle with chopped parsley and remaining grated cheese, if you please.

Two Iced Fruit Soups, Cinnamon Toast
4 little meals

If you lived in Eastern Europe, fruit soup would be an everyday occurrence. But you can make it a special treat, winter or summer, served chilled with warm cinnamon toast (see opposite). The colors range from pink to violet, depending on the season. Adorn winter soup with sour cream and toasted almonds, summer soup with yogurt and fresh mint.

Winter Plum

2 16-oz. cans purple plums, drained

1½ cups apple juice

1 cinnamon stick

3 thin orange slices

⅓ cup sour cream

1½ tsp. red wine vinegar

Freshly ground nutmeg

Pinch of salt

1. Pit plums. Put in food processor and purée until smooth.

2. In small saucepan, heat apple juice, cinnamon and oranges. Cook until reduced to 1 cup. Discard cinnamon and orange slices.

3. Put puréed plums in large bowl. Add apple juice mixture, sour cream, vinegar, nutmeg and salt. Mix and chill well. If too thick, add some water.

4. Serve with hot cinnamon toast.

Summer Plum

1½ lbs. fresh plums, red and purple

2 cups apple juice

1 cinnamon stick

1½ cups plain yogurt

Freshly ground nutmeg

1. Pit plums. Cut into chunks and put in pot with apple juice and cinnamon stick. Cook for 10 minutes until plums are very soft. Let cool. Remove cinnamon stick.

2. Purée plums and liquid in food processor until smooth. Put contents in bowl and stir in yogurt. Add nutmeg and mix until smooth. Chill well.

Cinnamon Toast

2½ tbsp. butter, melted

2 tsp. ground cinnamon

⅓ cup sugar

Pinch of ground ginger

4 slices firm white bread, crusts removed

1. Mix together butter, cinnamon, sugar and ginger to make a paste.

2. Toast bread.

3. Spread mixture on one side of bread.

4. Place on baking sheet. Bake in preheated 400° oven for 6 minutes.

Cherry Tomato Boboli

4 little meals

Love apples is another name for cherry tomatoes, and in fifteen minutes you can make a delicious compote to top a romantic little pizza. A touch of sweetness comes from apple jelly. Use fresh tarragon and Asiago cheese.

3 tbsp. vegetable oil

¼ cup finely chopped onion

1½ lbs. cherry tomatoes

1¼ tbsp. dried tarragon

2 tbsp. cider vinegar

1 tbsp. apple jelly

Salt and pepper to taste

2 seven-inch Bobolis

½ cup shredded Asiago cheese

1. Preheat oven to 500°.

2. Heat oil in large nonstick skillet, add onion and sauté until soft but not brown.

3. Add cherry tomatoes and cook over medium heat for 10 to 15 minutes until they get soft and burst open.

4. Add tarragon, vinegar, apple jelly, salt and pepper, and cook over high heat, pressing down on tomatoes. Cook for 5 minutes until the liquid has thickened.

5. Spread mixture over tops of Bobolis and sprinkle evenly with cheese. Bake on cookie sheet for 8 minutes. Cut in half and serve with a little salad or slices of crisp hickory-smoked bacon.

Carpaccio Gold

(chilled or pan-seared)

4 little meals

This dish was actually named after me (and the Italian painter) and appeared on a restaurant menu in New York for a decade. Paper-thin slices of raw beef are wrapped around a filling of mushrooms, Gruyère cheese and capers. If you don't like your beef raw, try it pan-seared.

8 oz. domestic mushrooms

3 oz. Gruyère cheese, julienned

1 tbsp. capers, drained

¼ cup minced scallions, white and green parts

3½ tbsp. olive oil

2½ tbsp. white wine vinegar

2 tsp. Dijon mustard

Salt and pepper to taste

¾ lb. beef tenderloin or sirloin, fat removed, sliced paper-thin

Coarse salt to taste

Arugula or dark romaine leaves

4 thin lemon wedges

Served chilled:

1. Slice mushrooms into thirds and then in half. Put into bowl with rest of ingredients except beef and lettuce and marinate for 30 minutes.

2. Line 4 plates evenly with thinly sliced beef. Put ½ cup mushroom salad in center of each and roll up into logs that are 2½ inches wide.

3. Brush top of each beef roll with olive oil, place several thin slices of mushrooms in center and sprinkle with coarse salt. Garnish with arugula or romaine and serve with a thin wedge of lemon.

Served warm:

1. Line 4 plates with arugula or romaine. Spread ½ cup mushroom salad in center of each.

2. Heat nonstick skillet and sear beef 10 seconds on each side. Put on top of salad and sprinkle with coarse salt.

Mussels from Brussels

2 little meals

The signature of Belgium, mussels are everywhere! Especially in Brussels, where we had our favorite rendition near the Grand' Place (Europe's most majestic town square). How wonderful to dine outdoors at midnight, wowed by a spectacular light show while dunking into these marvelous mollusks.

4 tbsp. butter

1 cup finely chopped onion

⅔ cup finely chopped celery

4 cloves minced garlic

¾ cup white wine

1 tbsp. herbs de Provence
(see **Note**)

2 tbsp. fresh thyme leaves (optional)

1 tsp. salt

2 lbs. mussels, scrubbed and debearded

2 tbsp. heavy cream

2 cup freshly chopped parsley

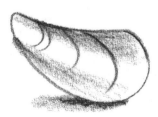

1. In large pot, melt butter and add onion, celery and garlic. Sauté until vegetables are soft but not brown.

2. Add wine, herbs and salt and bring to a boil.

3. Add mussels and cover pot. Shake pot back and forth and cook until mussels open, about 10 minutes.

4. Transfer mussels with slotted spoon to 2 soup bowls, discarding any that haven't opened. Add cream to pot and cook sauce over high heat until it has reduced and thickened slightly. Pour over mussels. Sprinkle with parsley.

Note: Or use a mixture of fennel seed, thyme and rosemary.

Autumn Breakfast

4 little meals

Imagine the aromas of gently spiced currant scones, hot from the oven, together with hickory-smoked bacon and simmering maple syrup. Use your favorite breakfast meats and pour a little syrup over everything, including the scones. This is also divine to serve at teatime after a walk in the woods.

Spiced Currant Scones:

2 cups all-purpose flour

½ tsp. salt

1 tsp. baking soda

2 tsp. cream of tartar

6 tbsp. sugar

¾ tsp. ground allspice

½ tsp. cinnamon

¼ tsp. ground ginger

4 tbsp. sweet butter

1 egg

⅔ cup buttermilk

½ cup currants

⅓ cup chopped walnuts, lightly toasted

1 egg yolk

1 tbsp. liqueur

½ lb. thick bacon

Your favorite breakfast sausage

Ham steak

Pure maple syrup, warmed

1. Preheat oven to 400°. Lightly grease a baking sheet.

2. In large bowl, sift together dry ingredients. Cut butter into the dry ingredients with two knives or a pastry blender until the mixture has a texture of coarse cornmeal.

3. In small bowl, mix together egg and buttermilk. Add slowly to flour mixture along with currants and walnuts. Mix gently until a soft dough is formed.

4. Put dough on floured board and pat into a 1-inch-thick circle.

5. Cut into 8 wedges and put on baking sheet. Glaze with egg yolk that has been mixed with 1 tbsp. of your favorite liqueur. Bake for 15 minutes or until lightly browned.

6. Cook meats until desired doneness. Serve with scones and warm maple syrup.

Japanese Custard in a Whole Red Pepper
4 little meals

Chawan-mushi is a savory custard much loved in Japan and traditionally baked in a lidded porcelain cup. I bake it in a whole red pepper for a very beautiful and edible presentation. You can add other ingredients, such as bits of chicken, water chestnuts or mushrooms. The delicate texture is firm but also a little soupy and is served with both chopsticks and a spoon.

½ lb. peeled medium shrimp

4 very large red bell peppers

½ cup cooked corn

¼ cup minced scallion, white part only

2 cups chicken broth

4 large eggs, beaten

1 tbsp. soy sauce

1 tbsp. dry sherry

¼ tsp. salt

6 tbsp. julienned basil leaves

1. Preheat oven to 425°.

2. Cook shrimp in boiling water for 30 seconds. Cut into ⅓-inch pieces.

3. Cut tops off peppers, reserve and take out seeds. Into each pepper evenly divide shrimp, corn and minced scallion.

4. In medium bowl, add broth to beaten eggs and mix well. Add soy sauce, sherry and salt. Beat gently with whisk.

5. Fill each pepper with egg mixture and top with 1½ tbsp. basil. Cover with pepper tops.

6. Put peppers in deep baking dish and add 1 inch of water. Bake for 35 minutes.

A Little Afternoon Tea
4 little meals

As executive chef of Lord & Taylor years ago, I was responsible for their restaurants nationwide. As many will remember, the Bird Cage was the place to go for dainty tea sandwiches and their famous chicken salad. It was also the place where men got two desserts! Here's their authentic recipe.

Classic Chicken Salad:

1¼ lbs. poached chicken breast (see page 17) in ⅓-inch dice

½ cup mayonnaise

½ cup sour cream

4 oz. finely chopped celery

1 tbsp. fresh lemon juice

¾ tbsp. finely minced onion

½ tsp. salt

¼ tsp. white pepper

1 recipe Lemon-Buttermilk Biscuits (see page 56), or thin-sliced white bread, crusts removed

½ cup chopped watercress

1 star fruit (carambola), sliced thin

Fresh sliced strawberries

1. Mix chicken with remaining salad ingredients and chill.

2. Make recipe for lemon-buttermilk biscuits. Cut into 8 2-inch rounds and bake.

3. Split biscuits and fill with chicken salad, putting 1 tbsp. chopped watercress on each.

4. Place 2 biscuits on each plate. Garnish with watercress, sliced star fruit and strawberries.

5. Serve with a pot of your favorite tea.

Sweet Baked Tomato

4 little desserts

A tomato is a fruit that becomes an exquisite dessert when made like a baked apple. It takes only 30 minutes to bake instead of the usual hour or more for the real McCoy. This dessert will surely become the apple of your eye.

4 large ripe tomatoes

½ cup currants

½ cup chopped walnuts

¼ cup sun-dried cranberries or golden raisins

2½ tbsp. honey

2 tsp. fresh lemon juice

½ tsp. ground cinnamon

¼ tsp. ground ginger

1½ cups apple juice

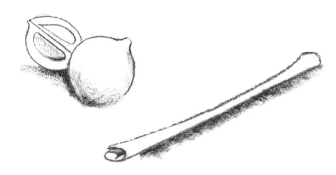

1. Preheat oven to 375°.

2. Slice tops off tomatoes and remove the insides, leaving shells intact. Turn upside down and drain on paper towels.

3. Mix together rest of ingredients except apple juice. Stuff tomatoes with this mixture.

4. Put tomatoes in deep baking dish and pour apple juice in bottom. Bake for 30 minutes.

5. Remove tomatoes with slotted spoon and chill. Reduce apple juice on top of stove until it becomes syrupy, then chill. Spoon sauce over tomatoes when serving.

Watermelon & Bitter Chocolate Salad

4 little desserts

Stolen from Kensington Place Restaurant, London, May 22, 1992.

4 cups very ripe watermelon, cut into thin 2-inch pieces

2-oz. chunk bitter chocolate or 2 1-oz. wrapped squares of unsweetened chocolate

1. The watermelon should be very ripe and intensely flavored. Remove seeds and chill.

2. Divide watermelon evenly into flat soup plates; cover tops with chocolate curls.

To make chocolate curls: Have chocolate at room temperature. With a vegetable peeler or small sharp knife, cut long, thin strips. The chocolate will form into curls or rolls. (If it is too cold, chocolate will flake; if too warm, it will smear.)

Chapter V

Low-Fat Little Meals

I created my first low-fat Little Meal in 1981 for Sophia Loren in the boardroom of Lord & Taylor. It was a trio of small, beautifully presented little dishes. It had a theme, it had harmony and it filled the senses, not the stomach: bejeweled oysters, shrimp and snow pea salad with red caviar, wine-poached pears with candied violets. Elegant repasts like these soon became my signature.

The challenge continued at the Rainbow Room when I was asked to develop two hundred low-calorie, low-sodium and low-cholesterol recipes for the fitness program called Evergreen. With the help of Joe Baum, Leslie Revsin and Richard Sax, we turned skeptics into believers and fat people into thin.

I learned, to my delight and fascination, that flavor had nothing to do with calories and fat, and eating healthfully had nothing to do with deprivation. Good nutrition had become as important as good taste, and our recipes had both.

The watchwords of today's cuisine have become *light, fresh* and *natural.* The salient characteristics of this low-fat odyssey are unusual flavor combinations, dramatic and artful presentations and organic, free-range ingredients, if possible. This new food consciousness stresses the benefits of grains, beans and vegetables, discourages the use of salt and sugar and decries the evils of fat.

The low-fat Little Meals that follow evoke flavors from all over the world. But, of course, this is not a new concept. In June 1958, *House & Garden* magazine featured "Low-Calorie Cookbook: Around the World in 80 Recipes," to "bring zest to your diet with foods, familiar and exotic, culled from the four corners of the world."

The culinary wheel continues to turn as we steam, grill, poach, spice and marinate ourselves into a healthy way of life.

These low-fat Little Meals are amazingly delicious—refreshing, elegant and easy to prepare. A range of worldly recipes includes chowder, chicken, steak, salmon and swordfish. Actually, there are lots of other low-fat dishes included in the book, but the recipes in this chapter are perhaps the most surprising, especially our low-fat desserts, including crème caramel and sticky pears.

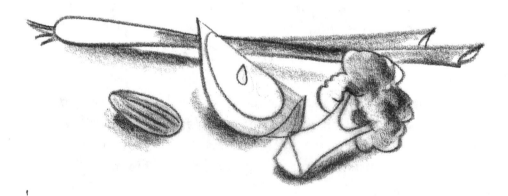

Couscous Chicken with Orange & Almonds, Yogurt Drizzle

4 little meals

Of the five hundred or more recipes I have created, I'm particularly fond of this one because it's exotic and simple at the same time. If you're making it for a VIP, serve with a chilled rosé champagne and follow with a pot of strong mint tea.

What's couscous? A processed fine-grain wheat, usually semolina, popular in North Africa. It looks like coarse yellow sand and is available in supermarkets and specialty-food stores.

1⅔ cups chicken broth

1 cup couscous

1 lb. skinless, boneless chicken breasts, poached and cooled (see page 17)

1 cup cooked chick-peas, drained

¾ cup sliced almonds

½ cup black raisins or currants

2 large oranges, peeled and segmented

½ cup finely chopped scallions

Dressing:

8 oz. plain yogurt

2 cloves garlic, pushed through garlic press

¼ cup fresh lemon juice

3 tbsp. olive oil

1 tsp. cumin powder

¼ tsp. salt

🖋

¼ cup plain yogurt

3 whole wheat pita breads, toasted and cut into triangles

95

1. Pour broth into medium saucepan and bring to a boil. Add cous-cous, stir, lower heat and cook until all broth is absorbed, about 10 minutes. Let cool.

2. Cut poached chicken into ½-inch strips. Put in large bowl with chick-peas, almonds, raisins, orange segments, scallions and cous-cous.

3. Mix together ingredients for dressing and pour over chicken mix-ture. Chill.

4. Divide salad evenly onto 4 plates. Drizzle with yogurt and serve with toasted whole wheat pita triangles.

Note: To make yogurt drizzle, mix yogurt with 1 tsp. water and put in squeeze bottle equipped with a fine tip. Cover and shake well.

Piperade Steak

4 little meals

Here is a perfect Little Meal for those who want their meat in small portions. Sirloin steak, in a zesty orange, fennel and peppercorn marinade, is seared rare and slightly chilled. Add black olives and a glass of light red wine for a Basque-style feast.

Dry Marinade:

3 garlic cloves, minced

3 shallots, thinly sliced

1 tsp. fennel seeds

1 tsp. dried rosemary leaves

1 tsp. dried thyme leaves

1 tsp. grated orange rind

1 tsp. black peppercorns, crushed

1 tbsp. balsamic vinegar

1 16-oz. sirloin steak

Piperade recipe, cold (see page 63)

4 fresh basil sprigs

12 oil-cured black olives

1. Mix together ingredients for marinade, then pour over steak. Let sit 2 to 3 hours.

2. Brush off dry marinade. Sear steak and cook until medium-rare. Chill slightly.

3. Mound piperade evenly onto 4 plates.

4. Slice steak on the diagonal ¼ inch thick and arrange slices on piperade. Garnish with basil sprigs and olives.

Mexican Corn & Rice Salad, Jumbo Shrimp

4 little meals

Jumbo shrimp is one of our favorite oxymorons! And this is one of our favorite dishes. Chopped green olives add piquancy to a confetti of brown rice. This is one of those rare times when a store-bought salsa does the trick, but don't tell anyone!

2 cups cooked brown rice

1 cup sweet corn kernels

½ cup finely chopped red bell pepper

½ cup finely chopped green bell pepper

¼ cup minced scallions

⅓ cup chopped pimento-stuffed olives

½ cup prepared salsa (mild or medium-hot)

3 tbsp. olive oil

Grated rind and juice of ½ lime

½ tsp. ground cumin

10 jumbo shrimp, peeled, cooked and chilled

4 large sprigs cilantro

1. In medium bowl, put brown rice, corn, red and green bell peppers, scallions and olives.

2. In small bowl, whisk together salsa, olive oil, lime rind and juice, and cumin. Pour over rice mixture and mix well. Chill.

3. Split shrimp to form 20 halves.

4. Divide rice salad evenly onto 4 plates. Pat each down into a 5-inch circle that is ¾ inch thick. Arrange halved shrimp in a circle on top of rice. Put a cilantro sprig in center.

Chicken Soup Live! (with Regis & Kathie Lee)

4 little meals

I've been told this was the world's best chicken soup, and it comes with amazing restorative powers. Regis and I had lots of fun when we made this together on television. We added matzoh balls for Passover (his were enormous!) and orzo, lemon and dill for Easter. Serve with matzoh or homemade zwieback (see opposite).

8 cups chicken broth	2 celery ribs, chopped
1 lb. chicken backs	1 turnip, chopped
1 red onion, chopped	2 cloves garlic, minced
2 leeks, chopped	2 tsp. dried basil leaves
3 carrots, chopped	¼ cup chopped fresh parsley

1. Put chicken broth in pot. Bring to a boil.

2. Add remaining ingredients. Lower heat, cover and cook 1 hour.

3. Remove chicken pieces and cook ½ hour. Skim any fat.

4. Optional: Add 8 matzoh balls (your favorite recipe) or 2 cups cooked orzo with juice of 1 lemon and ¼ cup chopped fresh dill.

Zwieback
(twice-baked bread)

Small loaf of unsliced white bread

1. Slice bread into ½-inch-thick slices.

2. Place on baking sheet and put in 200° oven to dry, leaving oven door open a little.

3. Raise temperature to 275°, close oven door and let brown lightly.

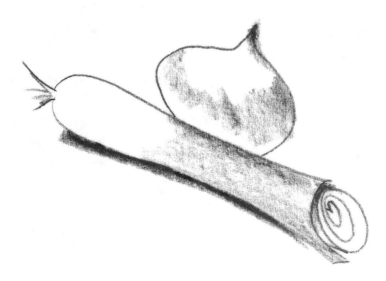

The $2 Little Meal

4 little meals

My husband and I have a funny routine when we make dinner. We're usually so exhausted after work that we don't go shopping, so we challenge each other to make a meal from whatever is in the house. This is the result of one very inexpensive "improv" dinner: caramelized onions and pasta.

2 tbsp. oil

1 ½ lbs. onions, thinly sliced

½ tsp. salt

½ tsp. sugar

1 tsp. dried basil leaves

½ tsp. dried thyme leaves

Freshly ground black pepper

½ cup water

2 tbsp. balsamic vinegar

12 oz. dried farfalle or bow-tie noodles

Grated Parmesan cheese (optional)

1. In large nonstick skillet heat oil. Add sliced onions and cook over high heat until onions begin to brown, about 10 minutes. If they begin to burn a little, that's okay.

2. Lower heat and add salt, sugar and spices. Cook 10 minutes, stirring often, until onions are uniformly caramel-colored. Add water and vinegar and cover. Simmer while pasta is cooking.

3. Meanwhile, in a separate pot, bring 3 quarts of water to a boil. Cook pasta according to directions. Drain well.

4. Divide pasta equally into 4 heated bowls. Top with equal portions of caramelized onions and sprinkle with grated Parmesan cheese, if desired.

Cumin Chicken on Pita Bread Salad

4 little meals

Never heard of bread salad? Two cuisines I can think of use leftover loaves as a salad ingredient. The Italians make *panzanella,* and Middle Easterners make *fattoush.* My creation mixes the refreshing flavors of tabbouleh with little cubes of pita bread, instead of the traditional bulgur wheat. Use as an edible oasis for moist cumin-rubbed chicken.

2 day-old 8-inch pita breads, toasted and cut into ⅓-inch dice

1 cup finely chopped fresh parsley

½ cup finely chopped scallions

⅓ cup finely chopped fresh mint

1 large ripe tomato, seeded and cut into ¼-inch dice

5 tbsp. fruity olive oil

3 tbsp. fresh lemon juice

½ tsp. salt

4 4-oz. chicken breasts, skinless and boneless

4 tsp. olive oil

2 tsp. ground cumin

Salt and freshly ground black pepper

Mint sprigs

1. In medium bowl, put diced pita bread, parsley, scallions, mint, tomato, olive oil, lemon juice and salt. Mix well and add 1 to 2 tbsp. cold water if dry. Cover and refrigerate ½ hour.

2. Coat each chicken breast with 1 tsp. olive oil. Rub cumin into top of each breast. Sprinkle lightly with salt and pepper. Grill or broil several minutes on each side.

3. To assemble: Arrange pita bread salad evenly on large plates to make 4-inch flat circles. Top with cumin chicken breasts. Garnish with fresh mint.

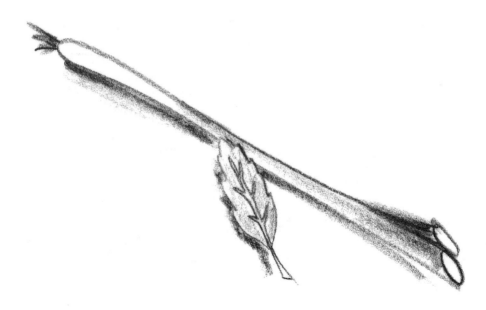

Warm Tomato "Cup" with Aromatic Couscous
4 little meals

Little grains of perfumed couscous fill this edible cup to make an extremely healthy Little Meal, low in calories, fat and cholesterol. This dish-for-all-seasons sits in a pool of lemon-scented broth. A basket of sesame-speckled lavash completes the repast.

4 large ripe tomatoes

1½ cups chicken broth, homemade or low-sodium canned

¼ cup canned tomato sauce

¼ cup minced carrot

¼ cup minced zucchini

2 cloves garlic, minced

½ tsp. ground cumin

½ tsp. ground coriander

¼ tsp. cinnamon

¼ tsp. cayenne pepper

¾ cup couscous

2 tbsp. finely chopped parsley

🌿

20 thin zucchini slices

¾ cup chicken broth

1 tbsp. fresh lemon juice

1. Cut ½ inch off tops of tomatoes and scoop out centers, leaving the shells. Turn upside down on paper towels to drain.

2. In pot put chicken broth, tomato sauce, minced vegetables and spices. Boil for 2 minutes.

3. Add couscous and lower heat. Cook 3 minutes or until most of the liquid is absorbed. Cover, turn off heat and let steam 2 minutes. Stir in parsley.

4. In 4 heatproof soup plates arrange zucchini slices in a circle. Put tomato in center and fill with ½ cup couscous.

5. Mix chicken broth and lemon juice and pour evenly around bottom of plates. Warm in 350° oven for 10 minutes.

Shrimp, Mango & Hearts of Palm
4 little meals

Juicy, ripe mangoes trigger vivid images of my grandparents' big, old mango tree in their West Palm Beach backyard. Up the street was a lime tree, and this dish is dedicated to fond childhood taste memories.

1 lb. large cooked shrimp, peeled

2 ripe mangoes

1 can hearts of palm, drained

½ cup fresh lime juice mixed with 1 tsp. catsup

1 tbsp. minced fresh jalapeño

¼ cup vegetable oil

Pinches of salt, sugar and black pepper

Fancy greens or leaf lettuce

4 thin lime slices

1. Cut shrimp into large dice and put in bowl.

2. Peel mangoes and cut into cubes the same size as the shrimp. Add to bowl.

3. Slice hearts of palm ⅓ inch thick and put in bowl.

4. Toss with lime juice, jalapeño, oil, and salt, sugar and pepper. Refrigerate 30 minutes.

5. Put lettuce on plates. Mound shrimp and mango salad in center and top each with a lime slice.

Pasta Rustica

4 little meals

The whole Mediterranean diet is rolled into one Little Meal: pasta, wine and olive oil. What else? Olives, garlic, lemon zest and low-fat fish. Perhaps the world's most perfect dish and easy to make, too. Serve with a crisp Italian white wine and some semolina bread.

¼ cup fruity olive oil

2 cloves garlic, minced

6 plum tomatoes, quartered and cut into ½-inch slices

3 tbsp. finely chopped fresh parsley

⅓ cup finely chopped fresh basil

1 tbsp. grated lemon rind

½ cup white wine

¾ lb. lemon or gray sole, cut into ½-inch strips

15 Kalamata olives, pitted and cut in half

1 tsp. salt

Freshly ground black pepper

½ lb. penne rigate (or other tubular pasta), cooked

2 tbsp. finely chopped fresh parsley

1. In a wok or large skillet, heat olive oil. Add garlic and cook over medium heat for 2 minutes. Do not brown.

2. Add tomatoes, parsley, basil, lemon rind and white wine. Cook 3 minutes over high heat.

3. Add fish, olives, salt and pepper. Cook 2 minutes until fish is just cooked.

4. Add cooked pasta and toss thoroughly with sauce.

5. Serve in 4 flat soup plates. Garnish with chopped parsley.

Succotash Chowder

4 hearty little meals

The horticulturally winning combination of sweet yellow corn and baby lima beans was borrowed from the Indians and traveled south from Succotash Point, Rhode Island, to kitchens in Dixie. It recently migrated to Brooklyn, New York, where it was turned into a chowder in my home kitchen. This hearty soup has only a trace of fat. Serve with a simple green salad and hot biscuits, if you wish.

1 cup finely chopped red onion

1 cup diced red pepper

2 cloves garlic, minced

½ tbsp. ground cumin

1 tsp. chile powder

4 cups chicken broth, homemade or low-sodium canned

½ lb. thin-skinned potatoes, washed and cut into ¼-inch dice

½ cup finely chopped cilantro

1 cup 1 percent milk

2 cups fresh or frozen corn

2 cups fresh or frozen baby lima beans, cooked

1. In large enamel pot, cook the onion, red pepper, garlic, cumin and chile powder in 1 cup chicken broth for 10 minutes until soft.

2. Add potatoes, 2 cups broth and cilantro. Cook until potatoes are almost done, about 15 minutes.

3. Add remaining 1 cup broth, milk and corn. Cook 10 minutes, then purée half of the soup in a food processor.

4. Pour puréed soup back into pot, add lima beans and cook 1 to 2 minutes until soup has thickened.

Chardonnay Chicken & Grapes on Minted Rice

4 little meals

This is a cousin of chicken Veronique, an Escoffier classic also made with grapes, but full of cream and butter. My version relies on a big, fruity white wine and spices for its flavor. Served with Minted White & Wild Rice (see page 114), it is *très elegante* and very low in calories.

1¼ lbs. chicken breasts, skinless and boneless

1 cup chardonnay

2 tbsp. fresh ginger, minced

2 cloves garlic, minced

1 small onion, thinly sliced

1½ tsp. ground cumin

½ tsp. ground coriander

½ tsp. powdered mustard

1 tsp. salt

¼ tsp. freshly ground black pepper

8 oz. seedless red or green grapes

1½ tbsp. olive oil

1 tbsp. sweet butter, cold

Mint sprigs

1. In medium bowl, marinate all ingredients, except olive oil, butter and mint sprigs, for 30 minutes.

2. Remove chicken from marinade. Reserve marinade.

3. Cut chicken breasts into ¾-inch-wide strips. Pat dry with paper towel.

4. In nonstick sauté pan, heat olive oil. Brown chicken on both sides. Add marinade (including grapes) and cook over high heat for 5 minutes until chicken is done. Whisk in cold butter until sauce thickens slightly.

5. Serve over ½ cup minted rice per person. Garnish with fresh mint sprigs.

Minted White & Wild Rice

1 cup water

1 cup chicken broth, homemade or low-sodium canned

⅛ tsp. black pepper

¾ cup white and wild rice blend

1½ tbsp. fresh mint, finely chopped

1. In medium saucepan, bring water, broth and pepper to a boil.

2. Add rice. Cover pot and cook over moderate heat for 25 to 30 minutes until water is absorbed and rice is tender.

3. Add freshly chopped mint. Mix well.

Seviche, Straight Up, with a Twist
4 little meals

This is a particularly delicious seviche made with scallops and halibut. But its real character comes from its presentation, served in frozen martini glasses with salt-encrusted rims. Nice with little bowls of green olives and almonds.

¾ lb. bay scallops

½ lb. halibut, cut into ½-inch cubes

½ green pepper, finely chopped

½ red pepper, finely julienned

¼ cup red onion, finely chopped

1 clove garlic, minced

3 tbsp. fresh cilantro, chopped fine

¼ cup fresh lime juice

½ cup fresh lemon juice

1 tbsp. olive oil

½ tsp. salt

Few drops Tabasco sauce

4 long strips lemon rind for garnish

1. In large bowl, mix all ingredients, except lemon rind, well. Chill for 2 to 3 hours.

2. Dip rims of 4 martini glasses in lemon juice and then in salt. Freeze until ready to use.

3. Divide seviche evenly into glasses and garnish with lemon rind twist.

Poached Salmon with Cucumber-Mint Frappé
4 little meals

Perfectly poached salmon, slightly rare in the center, sitting in a puddle of cool green sauce spiked with gin, is a summer Little Meal for "ladies who lunch." Serve with thinly sliced pumpernickel bread and a chilled fumé blanc.

Frappé:

1 cucumber, peeled and seeded

½ cup plain yogurt

1 tbsp. gin

1 clove garlic, pushed through garlic press

1½ tbsp. fresh mint, chopped

½ green pepper, chopped

¼ tsp. salt

4 3-oz. pieces salmon, poached and cooled

4 tsp. plain yogurt

4 mint sprigs

Pumpernickel bread, thinly sliced

1. Make sure all ingredients for frappé are very cold and put in food processor. Process until it becomes a smooth, frothy frappé.

2. Put ⅓ cup frappé in each of 4 well-chilled flat soup plates.

3. Place poached salmon in center. Garnish with 1 tsp. yogurt and a sprig of mint. Serve with pumpernickel bread.

Steamed Shrimp & Artichoke, Mustard Seed Dressing
4 little meals

To me, artichokes are the most precious of all the winter and early spring vegetables. Find globe or French artichokes with the longest stems possible because they're dramatic served upside down. When paired with silky steamed butterflied shrimp, artichoke becomes a chic Little Meal. Serve a wine with a touch of sweetness, like a Riesling from Alsace or a Chenin Blanc from California.

Dressing:

1 tbsp. Dijon mustard

1 tbsp. lemon juice

1 tbsp. white wine vinegar

⅓ cup olive oil

¾ tsp. mustard seeds

16 large shrimp

4 large artichokes with long stems

16 artichoke leaves, reserved

Escarole or leaf lettuce

2 plum tomatoes, cut into 8 wedges each

1. Mix ingredients for dressing and chill.

2. Peel shrimp, devein and butterfly. Steam 2 minutes over boiling water. Reserve.

3. Lay each artichoke on its side and, using a sharp knife, slice off top half and discard. Strip remaining leaves from base, reserving 16.

Remove center choke with spoon and peel the stem. Immediately cook artichoke hearts and reserved leaves in boiling water until tender, about 20 minutes. Drain well and chill.

4. To arrange salad, line plates with escarole or leaf lettuce. Place an artichoke in center of each, stem up. Place 4 shrimp evenly around the artichoke, alternating with 4 artichoke leaves. Place 1 tomato wedge inside each leaf. Drizzle everything with dressing.

Grilled Swordfish, Mango-Tomatillo Relish
4 little meals

Tomatillos are an indispensable ingredient in Mexican cuisine. They look like little green tomatoes but are really related to the gooseberry. Remove the papery husk and wash well. Low in fat and high in flavor, this swordfish dish is thoroughly trendy. Good for you and good-looking, too!

Mango-Tomatillo Relish:

3 limes, peeled, seeded and segmented (reserve juice)

⅔ cup diced tomatillo

⅔ cup diced mango

3 tbsp. finely diced red pepper

3 tbsp. finely diced yellow pepper

¼ cup chopped cilantro

4 swordfish fillets, cut into 5-oz. portions

Salt and white pepper

Fresh chives, cut into ½-inch lengths

1. Mix ingredients for relish and toss with a little of the reserved lime juice. Chill.

2. Sprinkle both sides of swordfish with salt and white pepper. Cook fish so that it's juicy in the center: grill outdoors, broil or pan-sear.

3. Serve hot with cold mango relish. Scatter chives on top.

Beet & Fennel Borscht, Boiled Potato
4 little meals

There are almost as many borscht variations as there are characters in a Tolstoy novel. But the central ingredient is always the voluptuous crimson beet. This Ukrainian soup is even more delicious the next day and should be served piping hot. It's hard to believe that something so low in calories, fat and sodium could be so full of flavor. Serve with a basket of coarse black bread or crunchy flat breads.

½ lb. peeled and trimmed beets

4 cups chicken broth, homemade or low-sodium canned

1 cup finely chopped red onion

2 carrots, minced

1 cup coarsely chopped fennel

1 tsp. caraway seeds

½ tsp. ground allspice

½ tsp. fennel seeds

Freshly ground black pepper

½ tbsp. red wine vinegar

¼ cup finely minced dill

4 medium potatoes, peeled and cooked

1 cup nonfat plain yogurt

½ cup peeled, seeded and diced cucumber

1. Cut beets into ¼-inch dice.

2. In large enamel pot with cover, put beets, broth, onion, carrots, coarsely chopped fennel, caraway, allspice, fennel seeds and pepper.

3. Cover and cook over medium heat for 45 minutes.

4. Uncover, add vinegar and dill and cook an additional 15 minutes.

5. Serve in soup bowls with boiled potato in center. Serve with small dishes of nonfat plain yogurt and seeded, diced cucumber, if desired.

99-Calorie Crème Caramel
6 little desserts

Yes, it's true.

6 tbsp. plus 2½ tbsp. sugar

2 cups 1 percent milk

1 whole egg and 2 egg whites

½ tsp. vanilla extract

⅛ tsp. almond extract

½ tsp. freshly grated orange rind

1. Preheat oven to 350°.

2. Melt 6 tbsp. sugar in small nonstick pan to caramelize. After 2 to 3 minutes, the sugar will become a dark brown syrup. Pour evenly into 6 custard cups.

3. Scald milk in saucepan.

4. In bowl, beat eggs with 2½ tbsp. sugar. Add milk slowly, whisking constantly. Add vanilla and almond extracts and orange rind. Let sit 10 minutes.

5. Pour mixture into custard cups. Place cups in a deep pan. Pour boiling water in pan until it reaches halfway up the sides of the cups. Bake for 40 to 45 minutes. Remove from water bath and refrigerate until very cold.

6. Run knife around edges of cups. Turn upside down on large plates. Custard will come out easily and caramel will form a sauce around the custard.

Note: For espresso crème caramel, add 3 tbsp. instant espresso after the scalded milk has been added to the eggs.

Sticky Pears, Maple-Nut Sauce
4 little desserts

Cold, lemony poached pears are covered with a crunchy-sticky maple-nut sauce that is the consistency of molten taffy. A remarkable study of tastes and textures! (The sauce is also great on coffee ice cream.)

4 large Bartlett pears, with long stems

1½ qts. water

½ cup sugar

1 cinnamon stick

5 lemon slices

Maple-Nut Sauce:

1 cup pure maple syrup

2 tsp. lemon juice

5 tbsp. chopped walnuts

1. Peel pears, leaving stems intact. Cut thin slice from bottoms so that pears will stand erect.

2. In medium pot, bring water, sugar, cinnamon and lemon to a boil. Lower heat, add pears and cover. Cook for 1 hour or until pears are tender.

3. Let pears cool in liquid and refrigerate for several hours.

4. Cook maple syrup and lemon juice in enamel saucepan over low heat. Reduce to ¾ cup. Add chopped nuts and keep warm.

5. Remove pears from liquid with slotted spoon. Put 1 pear on each plate and spoon hot sauce over.

Chapter VI

Speed and Ease

I became the fastest cook alive while spokesperson for the National Pasta Association. I learned the necessity of a well-stocked larder and a kitchen timer as I demonstrated "Pasta Improv" on scores of television shows around the country.

My prop table was set with ingredients that you would typically have at home, including a bowl of pasta, cooked al dente. The challenge of this Pasta Improv madness was to create a delicious Little Meal out of anything the TV host wanted to include in the dish. After only *two minutes* I could make a delectable cold pasta salad and a hot pasta creation, stir-fried in my electric wok!

For most of us, the desire to cook is related to the time available. If the truth be told, every time we feed our family or entertain friends, we go through ten steps before we complete the task:

1. Think about what to serve (sometimes this takes days if you're anything like me).

2. Find appropriate recipes or create your own.

3. Shop for the food.

4. Prep the food.

5. Cook the food.

6. Set the table.

7. Serve the food.

8. Serve the wine (or other beverage).

9. Clear the table.

10. Clean up.

So cooking may be only a small part of the total effort.

Some recipes in this chapter are just plain quick and easy, but many represent trade-offs of speed versus simplicity of preparation. You'll find several that require a fair amount of mixing and chopping, but then they're assembled in an instant; others may have few ingredients to deal with but need more time in the skillet. None is technically complex and (I promise) none will keep you long in the kitchen. These are good busy-day recipes; they all take under thirty minutes.

I've also included a list of lightning-fast and perfectly simple Little Meals for all you sixty-second gourmets.

60-Second Little Meals

Jam and bread, hot tea

Soft-boiled egg and whole wheat toast

A good ham sandwich

Prosciutto and melon, Parmesan curls

Avocado bread: mashed avocado with oil, vinegar and pepper
on white bread

Fried egg Mexicana: fried egg, salsa, corn tortilla

Honey and peaches in yogurt, raisin bread toast

Apple, farmhouse Cheddar and whole walnuts

Dutch breakfast: bread, butter and chocolate shavings

Herring smørrebrød, cucumber and dill

Leaning Tower of Mozzarella (see page 146)

Sliced yellow tomatoes on grilled peasant bread, fresh mint
and coarse salt

Japanese soup: chicken broth, diced bean curd,
watercress, dash of mirin

Stilton, grapes, biscuits and port

Caponata from a can, goat cheese and extra-virgin olive oil

Toasted pita bread, feta cheese,
olives and cucumber with mint tea

Champagne and caviar

Apple cider and doughnuts

Omelet and a glass of wine

Smoked Salmon Boboli

4 little meals

A Boboli is a big, puffy round of dough somewhere between bread and pizza crust. It is also similar to focaccia, a flat, unadorned Italian bread, predecessor to the pizza. Here it is used as a base for a smear of cream cheese and sour cream draped with smoked salmon. Serve with a green salad for a splendid repast.

2 seven-inch Boboli breads

3 oz. cream cheese, softened

2 tbsp. sour cream

1 small red onion, thinly sliced

6 oz. smoked salmon

4 oz. fresh mozzarella

2 tsp. grated Parmesan

2 tbsp. chopped scallions

🖋

Cherry tomatoes (optional)

Black olives (optional)

1. Spread each Boboli with cream cheese, then spread sour cream evenly over cream cheese.

2. Top each with 6 to 8 overlapping onion rings and cover evenly with smoked salmon.

3. Sprinkle with mozzarella, Parmesan and scallions.

4. Bake in 450° oven for 4 minutes, then put under broiler for 15 seconds.

5. Cut in half for 4 Little Meals. Serve with sliced cherry tomatoes and a few black olives, or with a green salad.

"Green Eggs 'n' Ham"
4 little meals

A tribute to Dr. Seuss, whose book we all loved as children. As an adult you'll adore this sophisticated Little Meal whose green herbs taste of springtime itself. Serve with fingers of lightly buttered whole wheat toast. Read the book out loud.

2½ cups herbs (any combination of watercress, cilantro, scallions, basil, parsley, mint)

8 large eggs

2 tbsp. water

1 tbsp. grated Parmesan cheese

2 tbsp. chilled sweet butter, cut into little pieces

Salt and freshly ground black pepper

½ lb. prosciutto, thinly sliced

4 slices of your favorite toast, lightly buttered

1. In food processor, put herbs and process until finely minced. Reserve.

2. In medium bowl, whisk eggs and water until fluffy.

3. Stir in herbs and Parmesan cheese.

4. Rub cold nonstick pan with 1 tsp. butter. Add eggs and heat over low flame.

5. Using a soft spatula, stir the eggs, periodically adding pieces of butter as eggs start to set. Lower the heat or the eggs will get rubbery, and continue adding pieces of butter, stirring and scraping bottom of pan with increasing frequency. Add salt and pepper.

Note: Add salt at the end because it toughens the protein of the egg.

6. To assemble: Line each of 4 plates with 2 oz. prosciutto. Place equal mounds of eggs in center of plate. Serve with buttered toast.

Do-It-Yourself Guacamole Kit

4 little meals

Only some like it hot, so this Little Meal puts each person in charge! The colors are like an artist's palette: Cool vegetables and spicy jalapeños surround a mound of perfectly ripe chunky avocado. Serve with warm tortilla chips and a cocktail shaker of margaritas.

4 very ripe avocados

Juice of 2 lemons

Salt and cayenne pepper to taste

½ cup chopped scallions

½ cup chopped cilantro

½ cup minced red onion

½ cup minced red pepper

½ cup minced yellow or green pepper

½ cup chopped tomato

¼ cup minced fresh jalapeño

Warm tortilla chips

1. Coarsely mash avocados in large bowl. Add lemon juice, salt and pepper to taste.

2. Mound avocado in center of each plate. Surround with 2 tbsp. of each of the garnishes.

3. Place tortilla chips on baking tray and put in oven to warm. Serve in individual baskets.

Filet Mignonettes,
Celery Sticks & Blue Cheese Dressing
4 little meals

Here's a steakhouse experience in a Little Meal. Derived from Buffalo chicken wings, these nuggets of seared filet mignon provide a big taste explosion when tossed with hot sauce and melted butter. Pair with chunky blue cheese dressing and ice-cold celery sticks and you will have a new "classic" combo.

Blue Cheese Dressing:

½ cup mayonnaise

½ cup sour cream

2½ tbsp. distilled white vinegar

4 oz. blue cheese, crumbled

¼ tsp. salt

🖋

1¼ lbs. filet mignon, cut into ¾-inch cubes

3 tbsp. hot sauce

3 tbsp. salted butter, melted

🖋

24 celery sticks (or more)

1⅓ cups blue cheese dressing

1. To make dressing: Put all ingredients for dressing in bowl and mix well. Refrigerate.

2. Lightly brush frying pan with oil. When pan is hot add filet mignon and brown well, leaving inside rare.

3. Put hot sauce and butter in bowl. When meat is cooked, add to bowl and toss well.

4. Divide filet mignon evenly onto plates. Serve with celery sticks, ramekins of dressing and more hot sauce, if desired.

Jumbo Shrimp Cocktail "On the Rocks"

4 little meals

Freezing turns jarred cocktail sauce into a wondrous quick sorbet, so serving shrimp "on the rocks" is more than just a kicky idea: The rocks keep the red sauce from thawing quickly and give new meaning to a shrimp "cocktail." Also a great look-at-me first course for an elegant dinner.

8 oz. cocktail sauce, frozen in jar

1 cup ice cubes

Flat parsley sprigs

1 cup shredded iceberg lettuce

4 lemon wedges

20 jumbo shrimp, cooked and chilled

Oyster crackers or common crackers

1. Put frozen cocktail sauce in food processor. Blend until it is the consistency of sorbet.

2. Divide ice cubes among 4 large old-fashioned glasses. Cover with shredded lettuce. Place 5 shrimp around the edge of each glass.

3. Using an ice cream scoop, place cocktail sauce on top of lettuce. Garnish with parsley.

4. Set "cocktails" on doily-lined plates with a lemon wedge and crackers.

Gorgonzola & Polenta Melt, Arugula Julienne
4 little meals

I remember a dish like this from Tuscany in my youth. The texture and aroma of a perfectly ripened Gorgonzola cheese is unforgettable. Use a real one imported from Italy or substitute a nutty, room-temperature Fontina. Creamy, hot polenta and cool, astringent arugula laced with balsamic vinegar are a winning combination.

Polenta:

4 cups water

½ tbsp. salt

¾ cup yellow cornmeal

1 bunch arugula, julienned

1 tbsp. olive oil

½ tbsp. balsamic vinegar

10 to 12 oz. ripe Gorgonzola cheese, at room temperature

1. Bring water and salt to a boil in medium pot and add cornmeal very slowly, stirring often. Cook for 25 minutes until polenta is smooth and thick.

2. In small bowl toss arugula with olive oil and vinegar.

3. Divide cheese evenly onto 4 plates. Put dressed arugula next to cheese. Pour ½ cup hot polenta over center of cheese.

Grilled Chorizos, Jicama-Orange Salad

4 little meals

Jicama is a wonderfully crunchy tuber from Mexico. When cut like straw potatoes, it becomes an edible bed for warm, spicy chorizo drippings that mingle with fresh citrus juices. If you can't find Spanish chorizos, use Italian pepperoni.

1 lb. jicama

¾ lb. chorizo or pepperoni

2 large oranges, peeled and segmented

¼ cup fresh lemon juice

2 tsp. paprika

4 large fresh parsley sprigs

1. Peel jicama and cut into matchstick julienne. Reserve.

2. Cut chorizo or pepperoni into ½-inch-thick slices. Broil 2 to 3 minutes on tray until browned. Keep warm.

3. Divide jicama evenly onto 4 plates and top each portion with 5 orange segments. Sprinkle with 1 tbsp. fresh lemon juice.

4. Place 6 to 7 slices of chorizo with drippings on top of each salad. Sprinkle with ½ tsp. paprika and garnish with a parsley sprig in the center.

King Crab, Grapefruit & Avocado Salad, Chile-Lime Dressing

4 little meals

A refreshing southwestern-style Little Meal for any time of year. Use king crab legs any way you can find them—in the shell or out. Serve with a basket of warm tortillas.

2 ripe avocados

2 grapefruits

1 lb. king crab legs

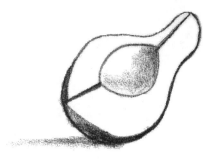

Small bunch cilantro

¼ cup minced red bell pepper

Chile-Lime Dressing:

¼ cup melon liqueur (see **Note**)

Grated rind of 1 lime

¼ cup fresh lime juice

2 tsp. mild chile powder

1 scallion, cut into 1-inch pieces

½ tsp. salt

½ cup corn oil

1. Peel avocados and cut in half. Slice each half into 5 segments.

2. Peel grapefruits and cut into segments.

3. Overlap 5 slices of avocado and grapefruit on each of 4 large plates. Top each with ¼ lb. king crab. Garnish with cilantro and minced red pepper.

4. To make dressing: In food processor, put melon liqueur, grated lime rind, lime juice, chile powder, scallion and salt. Process until smooth. Slowly add corn oil. Dressing should thicken slightly. Chill.

5. Pour dressing evenly over salads.

Note: If you don't have melon liqueur, substitute with ¼ cup fresh orange juice mixed with 2 tsp. honey.

Seared Salmon on a Moroccan Salad
4 little meals

Red onion, orange and black olive salad can be found from North Africa to Sicily. But never has it been found with seared salmon on top and draped with black olive vinaigrette. It's dazzling.

¼ cup Black Olive Paste (see page 59)

2 tbsp. water

2 tbsp. olive oil

4 small oranges, peeled and cut into ⅓-inch-thick slices

1 small red onion, thinly sliced

4 3-oz. salmon filets

1. In small bowl, loosen olive paste with water and add olive oil. Blend until smooth.

2. On 4 plates, arrange orange slices with red onions on top.

3. Get nonstick skillet very hot. Sear salmon on both sides so that the outside is crisp and the inside is pink. Remove from pan and set aside.

4. Place salmon in center of each salad. Drizzle black olive dressing over the salmon and around the edges of the salad.

Barcelona Bread

4 little meals

I call this Barcelona Bread; however, more official names include *Pan Catalán* and *Pa Amb Tomàquet*. One finds it wherever one goes in that city, at home and in fancy restaurants. Our favorite version was served with local sausages, perfumed Jabugo ham and green olives the size of golf balls. Try it at home with fried eggs and finish with a dry fino sherry.

8 large 1-inch-thick slices stale peasant bread

2 large cloves garlic, cut in half

2 large, very ripe tomatoes, cut in half

Fruity olive oil

Sea salt

4 eggs, fried sunny side up

¼ cup finely chopped parsley

4 slices prosciutto or several slices grilled chorizo sausage

1. Toast bread under broiler until lightly browned on both sides.

2. Rub one side of each slice with cut garlic clove.

3. Rub tops of bread with cut tomato, soaking with tomato seeds and juice over entire surface. Drizzle olive oil on both sides and sprinkle with sea salt.

4. Serve 2 slices of bread per person. Add eggs, chopped parsley and prosciutto or sausage.

Tomato "Benedict"

4 little meals

No eggs, no hollandaise, no ham. But there are two Holland rusks with fat, ripe tomatoes spread with olive paste and capped with bubbling mozzarella. Top with black olive halves instead of black truffles. A drizzle of balsamic vinegar becomes your sauce.

8 Holland rusks

2 large, ripe tomatoes

3 tbsp. Black Olive Paste
(see page 59)

1 lb. fresh mozzarella

½ lb. spinach leaves,
½ cup julienned

4 black olives, halved

2 tbsp. balsamic vinegar

1. Put rusks on baking sheet.

2. Cut tomatoes into 8 thick slices. Spread with olive paste. Put on top of rusks.

3. Cut mozzarella into 8 ½-inch-thick slices. Put on top of tomatoes.

4. Broil until melted and lightly brown.

5. To serve: Put spinach leaves on 4 plates. Place 2 rusks on top of each. Garnish with black olive halves and a tablespoon of julienned spinach. Drizzle with ½ tbsp. vinegar.

Leaning Tower of Mozzarella

4 little meals

Simplicity itself. The red, white and green colors remind me of the Italian flag. Use fresh, snow-white mozzarella cheese from your local Italian deli. A splash of extra-virgin olive oil and coarse salt complete your dish. Serve with Italian bread, of course.

4 large, ripe tomatoes with stem, if possible

1 lb. fresh mozzarella

1 cucumber

4 large basil sprigs

¼ cup extra-virgin olive oil

1. Cut each tomato into 4 thick slices.

2. Cut mozzarella into 12 ½-inch-thick slices.

3. Cut cucumber into 12 ¼-inch-thick slices with skin left on.

4. Arrange tomato, cheese and cucumber in an overlapping row across each plate. Each portion should have 4 tomato slices and 3 slices each of cheese and cucumber. Garnish with a large basil sprig and 1 tbsp. olive oil.

BLT Quesadilla, Triple-Decker
4 little meals

A Little Meal from Mexico. Triple-decker quesadillas are almost as much fun to eat as they are to make! Layer six-inch flour tortillas with shredded cheese and inventive fillings and bake in a hot oven. You will have an impressive Little Meal in less than ten minutes. A BLT quesadilla is suitable for B, L and T (breakfast, lunch and tea)!

Jalapeño Mayonnaise:

½ cup mayonnaise

1 tbsp. minced fresh parsley

1 tbsp. finely chopped canned jalapeño pepper

4 ripe tomatoes, sliced thin

16 slices cooked bacon

¾ lb. shredded cheese, Monterey Jack and Asiago mixed

Shredded lettuce

12 6-inch flour tortillas

1. Preheat oven to 425°.

2. Mix mayonnaise, parsley and jalapeños. Cover and put in refrigerator.

3. Layer each quesadilla bottom-up as follows:

> tortilla
>
> 4 slices tomato
>
> 2 slices bacon
>
> 1½ oz. cheese
>
> second tortilla
>
> 4 slices tomato
>
> 2 slices bacon
>
> 1½ oz. cheese
>
> third tortilla

Brush top lightly with oil.

4. Put on baking sheet and bake for 8 to 10 minutes until top is lightly browned.

5. Put 1 quesadilla on each plate. Cut in quarters. Place shredded lettuce in center and top with jalapeño mayonnaise.

Seafood Quesadilla, Triple-Decker
2 little meals

This triple-decker quesadilla has sophisticated flavors. It can be made with all manner of seafood, from chopped clams to smoked oysters. But it's also splendid with tiny cooked shrimp or lobster. The ricotta and assertive herbs will complement them all. A little squeeze of lemon is the final touch.

⅔ cup ricotta cheese

1 clove garlic, pushed through garlic press

6 6-inch flour tortillas

1 cup chopped cooked seafood (clams, smoked oysters, crab, shrimp, lobster)

1½ tbsp. small capers

1 tsp. fennel seed

1 small tomato, seeded and chopped

⅓ cup julienned basil leaves

6 oz. shredded cheese, Monterey Jack and Asiago mixed

Whole basil leaves

2 lemon slices, cut in half

1. Preheat oven to 425°.

2. Mix ricotta with garlic.

3. Layer each quesadilla bottom-up as follows:

> tortilla
>
> ⅓ cup ricotta cheese
>
> ½ cup seafood
>
> ¾ tbsp. capers
>
> ½ tsp. fennel seed
>
> second tortilla
>
> ½ chopped tomato
>
> 3 tbsp. julienned basil
>
> 3 oz. shredded cheese
>
> third tortilla

Brush top lightly with oil.

4. Put on baking sheet and bake for 8 to 10 minutes until top is lightly browned.

5. Put 1 quesadilla on each plate. Cut in quarters. Garnish the center of each with basil leaves and 2 lemon slices.

Fried Green Tomatoes, Rosemary Mayonnaise

4 little meals

The famous movie revived my interest in green tomatoes, a fruit of distinctive flavor and texture. Cornmeal provides a coat of many crunches. Try them alone or in a sandwich. Watch the movie!

1 cup Rosemary Mayonnaise (see page 73)

2 plum tomatoes

4 large green tomatoes

2 eggs, beaten

¼ tsp. salt

1 cup cornmeal

¼ cup vegetable oil

¼ cup finely chopped parsley

1. Make 1 recipe of rosemary mayonnaise. Cut plum tomatoes in half and scoop out and discard center. Finely chop remaining shell. Mix with mayonnaise and chill.

2. Trim tops and bottoms of green tomatoes. Cut each into 3 thick slices. Dip in beaten eggs mixed with salt. Dredge tomatoes thoroughly in cornmeal.

3. Heat oil and fry tomatoes on both sides until golden brown.

4. Serve 3 overlapping slices for each portion. Put a large dollop of mayonnaise on top and garnish with parsley.

5. Serve with a cruet of white vinegar and extra rosemary mayonnaise on the side. (A basket of freshly made drop biscuits would be a lovely addition.)

RRBBLT

4 little meals

As restaurant consultants we created one of New York's busiest and bustling bars, overlooking the Hudson River. It's where everyone from the Stock Exchange and the World Financial Center goes after work. At the Edward Moran Bar & Grill you drink buckets of beer and eat RRBBLTs. Rare roast beef, bacon, lettuce and tomato, of course!

BBQ Mayonnaise:

1 cup mayonnaise

¼ cup barbecue sauce

🖎

12 slices rye bread with seeds

Leaf or romaine lettuce

¾ lb. thinly sliced rare roast beef

¾ cup French fried onions, canned

12 slices ripe tomato

8 slices cooked thick bacon, crisp

1. In small bowl mix mayonnaise and barbecue sauce.

2. For each sandwich: On bottom piece of bread put 1½ tbsp. BBQ mayonnaise. Top with lettuce, 3 oz. roast beef, 3 tbsp. fried onions, second slice of bread, 1½ tbsp. BBQ mayo, lettuce, 3 slices tomato, 2 slices bacon and cover with bread.

3. Stick 2 skewers in each sandwich and cut in half.

4. Serve with extra BBQ mayonnaise and warm potato chips or skinny French fries.

Pastina in Garlic Broth

3 to 4 little meals

Pastina is a tiny star-shaped pasta that you may recall, with nostalgia, from your youth. Here it is served forth as a gentle but very elegant Little Meal: soup and pasta in one dish, ultimately satisfying with oozing cheese and a splash of lemon juice.

2 qts. water

½ tbsp. salt

6 oz. pastina

3 cups chicken broth

2 cloves garlic, pushed through garlic press

½ cup shredded Asiago or white Cheddar cheese

¼ cup julienned fresh basil

3 tbsp. fruity olive oil

2 small lemons, cut in half

1. Bring water and salt to a boil. Add pastina, return to boil, stir and cook 5 minutes. Drain well and reserve.

2. In medium pot bring chicken broth to a boil. Lower heat, add garlic to broth. Simmer for 20 minutes until broth is reduced to 2 cups. Add cooked pastina and heat thoroughly.

3. Serve in large, flat soup plates. Put cheese and basil in center. Drizzle with olive oil and serve with lemon halves on the side.

Tennessee Doughnuts & Ham Steak
4 little meals

My father, a football star and war hero, is also a terrific cook. His specialties: boiled lobster, the world's best tuna salad and griddled doughnuts. Yes, he finds the biggest glazed yeast doughnuts he can and cooks them in a skillet, pressing down and flipping them like pancakes. Try several with a broiled ham steak. Wash down with a thermos of coffee.

Large ham steak

2 tbsp. butter

4 to 8 large glazed doughnuts (yeast-raised)

1. Broil ham steak on both sides. Keep warm.

2. In large nonstick skillet, melt 1 tbsp. butter. Put in 2 doughnuts and press down with spatula. Let brown and caramelize lightly on one side, then turn over and brown on the other side.

3. Remove from pan and keep warm in oven. Melt 1 tbsp. butter and repeat process.

4. Cut ham steak in equal portions and serve with 1 to 2 doughnuts for each person. Serve with a little warm syrup if needed.

Goat Cheese & Lemon Curd, Fresh Raspberries
4 little desserts

Lillian and Miles Cahn are mom and pop to six hundred "kids" at Coach Farms, where, in upstate New York, they produce delicious goat cheese. Great hosts, they also serve this charming Little Meal/dessert with chilled white wine from nearby Clinton Vineyards.

Lemon Curd:

3 tbsp. unsalted butter

¼ cup super-fine sugar

2 large lemons, grated rind and juice

1 large egg

½ lb. fresh goat cheese log

1⅓ cups fresh raspberries

English water crackers

Fresh herbs for garnish

1. Cream butter and sugar together in mixer.

2. In heat-proof bowl, beat together lemon rind, juice and egg. Add to butter mixture and stir until smooth.

3. Put in double boiler over hot water and whisk constantly until mixture has thickened. Refrigerate.

4. To serve: On each plate put 2½-inch slices of goat cheese in center. Place raspberries on one side and lemon curd on the other. Serve with crackers and any sweet fresh herbs you may have: mint, lemon balm, lavender.

Musician's Dessert

4 little desserts

Postre del Músico from Barcelona is a simple dessert with a sweet story. It began as a dish for peasants (and traveling musicians), served in little terra-cotta plates accompanied by glasses of thick, sweet Moscatel. It continues today as a satisfying coda to a meal in Catalonia.

2 cups dried fruits and nuts (pine nuts, raisins, pecans, apricots)

Glass of sweet Moscatel

Espresso

1. Mix fruits and nuts and divide among 4 small plates.

2. Chill wine.

3. Make coffee.

Note: Malvasia, Vin Santo or any sweet muscat-based wine may be substituted.

Chapter VII

Slow-Cooked Little Meals

There's something old-fashioned about slow cooking. When asked about my favorite food, I always reply that it's anything that takes more than an hour to cook. I love what happens to chicken braised slowly in a covered pot; or the alchemy by which layers of Mediterranean vegetables, losing moisture from slow baking, are transformed into a delicious, intense pancake. I love what occurs when onions are cooked long enough to caramelize, when pasta is baked to a noisy, crunchy crust, when lamb riblets trade their liquid for a deep mahogany glaze.

What I call the "grill it and garnish it" school of cooking certainly has a place in today's culinary lexicon, but I crave slow cooking. It's why people have fallen in love again with food that is sensuous and giving.

Slow cooking doesn't mean that making a Little Meal will gobble up your time. No – it means that food cooks itself while you engage in other productive pleasures, such as setting the table or preparing dessert, or slow dancing.

Some techniques in this chapter date from Grandmother's day, when time was more available and people had more patience. I've harnessed these slow-cooking techniques to create contemporary Little Meals full of old-fashioned flavor that, I fear, we're otherwise in danger of losing.

* * *

An extra benefit of slow cooking is that, generally, these dishes take well to reheating, which suggests that you might want to double the quantities for use later on in the week.

A Little Chicken & Garlic Stew

4 little meals

A lusty bistro dish for supper in front of the fireplace. The garlic cloves get so soft that they become a kind of butter for your bread. Use some flavorful white wine (I like Alsatian) and serve the rest to your guests. Several warm, crusty baguettes are essential.

2 tbsp. olive oil

4 chicken legs, separated into drumsticks and thighs

25 garlic cloves, unpeeled

½ cup chopped parsley

½ cup chopped celery leaves

1½ tsp. dried tarragon leaves

½ tbsp. sea salt

1 cup dry white wine

½ tsp. allspice

Freshly ground white pepper

2 tbsp. chopped parsley

1. Place olive oil in a heavy pot that can be covered tightly.

2. Add all ingredients except parsley and mix well.

3. Cover pot and place in preheated 375° oven for 1½ hours. The chicken will not brown but will be very moist and the garlic "sauce" will be mild.

4. To serve: Divide chicken and garlic evenly onto 4 plates and sprinkle with parsley.

Pork Honey Buns, Chinese-style
4 little meals

Honey-glazed bread dough becomes a beehive for ground pork seasoned, Oriental-style, with scallions, sherry and sesame oil. Water chestnuts give crunch to the filling. In miniature these are unusual hors d'oeuvres. Use an aromatic wildflower honey.

Cabbage Salad:

½ small savoy cabbage

½ tbsp. sugar

¼ cup rice wine vinegar

¼ tsp. salt

1 tbsp. sesame oil

¼ tsp. red pepper flakes

Filling:

2 tsp. sesame oil

1 lb. ground pork

½ cup finely chopped scallions, white and green parts

1 cup finely chopped mushrooms

1½ tbsp. dark brown sugar

½ tsp. salt

½ cup finely chopped water chestnuts

½ tbsp. cornstarch dissolved in 2 tbsp. sherry

🖎

1 lb. frozen bread dough, thawed

¼ cup honey

1. Finely shred cabbage. Dissolve sugar in vinegar and pour with remaining ingredients for salad over cabbage. Toss well and refrigerate.

2. Preheat oven to 350°.

3. In nonstick skillet, put sesame oil, pork and scallions. Cook over high heat until pork is browned. Add remaining ingredients for filling and cook until mixture has thickened slightly.

4. Cut dough into 4 portions. On lightly floured board pat dough into circles. Put pork mixture in center of each and fold into packets, seam side down.

5. Place on baking sheet and brush tops with honey. Bake for 25 minutes and brush with honey again. Serve on top of cabbage salad.

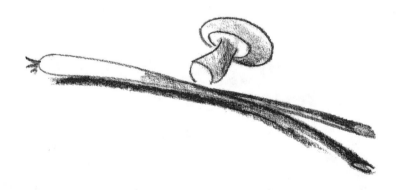

Rosemary-Lemon Chicken Wings

4 little meals

Move over, Buffalo; here's a Tuscan-style recipe for chicken wings bathed in olive oil, rosemary and garlic, resting on a bed of escarole. The marinade makes a quick dressing for the crunchy, bitter greens.

16 chicken wings
(approx. 2½ lbs.)

Marinade:

½ cup fruity olive oil

½ cup fresh lemon juice
(3 lemons)

3 bay leaves

3 tbsp. fresh rosemary leaves

5 cloves garlic, minced

2 tsp. sea salt

½ tsp. Tabasco sauce

Escarole leaves for lining plates

8 thin lemon slices

1. Remove wing tips and discard. Cut chicken wings in half.

2. In bowl put all ingredients for marinade.

3. Add chicken wings and cover. Refrigerate 4 to 6 hours or overnight.

4. Remove wings from marinade. Pat dry. Put on baking tray. Bake in preheated 400° oven for 25 minutes. Put under broiler for 5 minutes.

5. Heat the marinade just until it boils.

6. Line plates with freshly washed escarole. Pile 8 chicken pieces in center of each. Drizzle each plate with 2 tbsp. warm marinade and garnish with 2 lemon slices.

Sausage, Pepper & Olive Ragout

4 little meals

Great chefs have been making ragouts for centuries, but they never tasted like this before! My colorful stew is intensely flavored with sweet vermouth, fennel-infused sausages and saline green olives. After all, *ragoûter* means to stimulate the appetite!

1½ lbs. sweet Italian sausage

2 tbsp. olive oil

3 cloves garlic, thinly sliced

1¼ lbs. bell peppers—red, yellow and green—in ½-inch-thick strips

¼ tsp. salt

⅓ cup green olives

⅔ cup sweet vermouth

½ cup chicken stock

1 clove garlic, pushed through garlic press

½ tsp. hot pepper flakes

8 1-inch-thick slices Italian bread, toasted

Fresh basil leaves

1. Broil sausages until browned on all sides. Reserve.

2. In large nonstick skillet, heat olive oil and garlic. Do not brown.

3. Sauté peppers for 10 minutes until they begin to soften. Add salt and stir.

4. Cut sausages on bias into thick slices. Add to peppers along with olives and ⅓ cup of the vermouth. Cover and cook 10 minutes.

5. Remove cover and remove mixture with slotted spoon, leaving all juices in skillet. Put sausage mixture in bowl and keep warm.

6. Turn up heat under skillet. Add remaining vermouth, chicken stock, garlic and red pepper flakes and cook until sauce has reduced and thickened.

7. To serve: Place 2 slices toasted bread on each plate. Divide sausage mixture evenly and cover with sauce. Garnish with fresh basil leaves, if desired.

Philippine Vinegar Chicken
4 little meals

My cousin Rose discovered this recipe when she lived in the Philippines. Instead of using a whole chicken, as her recipe says, I hack up legs and thighs, Chinese-style. Cooked in vinegar and soy, the chicken turns mahogany and the juices become a dark, peppery syrup. An addictive Little Meal that will have you licking your fingers.

4 chicken legs (2½ lbs.)

1 medium onion, chopped

3 cloves garlic, minced

¼ cup white distilled vinegar

3 tbsp. soy sauce

20 black peppercorns

½ tsp. salt

¼ tsp. freshly ground black pepper

2 cups finely shredded bok choy

1. Hack chicken into 2-inch pieces using a cleaver or a very sharp, heavy knife.

2. Put in pot with remaining ingredients except bok choy. Cover and simmer 40 minutes.

3. Remove chicken with slotted spoon and keep warm. Reduce sauce by half over high heat.

4. Arrange bok choy evenly on plates. Top with chicken pieces and cover with sauce.

Cabbage & Noodles

4 little meals

My beautiful mother is of Hungarian descent, making her, of course, a wonderful cook. This was my favorite comfort dish growing up and needs nothing more than a glass of wine to accompany it. For a big meal, serve Palacsintas with Apricot Jam for dessert (see page 187).

1 large head green cabbage	1 medium onion, thinly sliced
1 tbsp. salt	12 oz. egg noodles, medium-wide
1 stick unsalted butter	Freshly ground black pepper

1. With a sharp knife, cut cabbage into ¼-inch slices. Place in large bowl and sprinkle with salt. Cover with a plate to weigh it down and refrigerate overnight. The next day, turn cabbage into a colander and squeeze dry.

2. In large pan, melt butter and add onion and cabbage. Sauté until mixture is golden brown and very soft.

3. Cook noodles according to package directions. Drain.

4. Toss noodles with cabbage mixture and add lots of freshly ground black pepper. Serve with fresh rye bread with caraway seeds.

Orzo "Risotto" with Wild Mushrooms

4 little meals

Risotto is an elegant Italian rice dish. My version, made with orzo (a rice-shaped pasta), uses the risotto technique of incorporating broth very slowly to produce a creamy yet nubby texture. Flavored with wild mushrooms and cognac, it's gourmet heaven. And unlike rice, orzo reheats beautifully with two tablespoons of water.

3 tbsp. olive oil

⅓ cup finely chopped shallots

¾ lb. orzo, uncooked

2 tbsp. cognac

3½ to 4 cups beef broth

4 oz. shiitake mushrooms, stems removed, thickly sliced

⅓ cup heavy cream

¼ cup grated Parmesan cheese

2 tbsp. finely chopped fresh parsley

1. In large enameled pot heat oil. Add shallots and cook until soft. Add orzo and sauté 5 minutes, stirring until golden brown.

2. Add cognac and let liquid evaporate.

3. Add 1 cup beef broth and cook over low heat until liquid is absorbed. Adjust heat as necessary and stir continuously with wooden spoon. Add next cup of broth and continue stirring.

4. Place mushrooms in pot and add remaining broth. Continue to cook until all broth is absorbed and orzo is tender.

5. Add cream, stir until heated and mix in cheese.

6. Divide evenly onto 4 plates and sprinkle with parsley. Pass the pepper mill and a small bowl of Parmesan cheese.

Orange-Ginger Lamb Riblets

4 little meals

These slow-barbecued riblets have a pungent sweet-and-sour glaze that turns an inexpensive cut of meat into the ultimate finger food. Serve with little baked sweet potatoes for a very interesting combination.

1 cup orange juice

⅔ cup hoisin sauce

3 tbsp. honey

¼ cup soy sauce

1 tbsp. Dijon mustard

4 cloves garlic, minced

¼ cup minced fresh ginger

3 lbs. lamb riblets (cut into individual ribs by butcher)

Watercress and orange wedges for garnish

1. Combine orange juice, hoisin sauce, honey, soy sauce, Dijon mustard, garlic and ginger and mix well. Pour over ribs. Marinate ribs several hours or overnight in refrigerator.

2. Preheat oven to 325°. Remove ribs from marinade and, setting marinade aside, place ribs on broiler pan fitted with a rack. Cover tightly with aluminum foil and bake for 45 minutes.

3. Heat marinade in saucepan until it thickens slightly.

4. Remove aluminum foil and bake another 45 minutes, basting ribs frequently with marinade, using a pastry brush.

5. Serve ribs with watercress, oranges and remaining marinade in little ramekins.

"Couch Potatoes"

4 little meals

Staying home and chilling out? This spud's for you. These are the best stuffed baked potatoes you will ever eat. One makes a Little Meal, or have two with a green salad for a bigger Little Meal. The mayo-ricotta topping resembles a cheese soufflé!

4 large baking potatoes

½ lb. broccoli florets

¼ lb. smoked ham, 1 thick slice

¼ lb. turkey, 1 thick slice

⅓ cup mayonnaise

Freshly ground black pepper

Leaf lettuce or salad greens

Topping:

½ cup mayonnaise

½ cup ricotta cheese

½ cup grated Parmesan cheese

1 clove garlic, pushed through garlic press

1. Scrub potatoes and bake at 400° for 50 minutes.

2. Meanwhile, cut florets into small pieces and blanch in boiling water for 3 minutes. Rinse under cold water and drain well. Put in bowl.

3. Dice ham and turkey into ¼-inch cubes and add to broccoli with ⅓ cup mayonnaise and freshly ground pepper.

4. When potatoes are done, cut them in half, scoop out half the insides and add potato pieces to broccoli mixture. Mix well.

5. Stuff potato halves with mixture.

6. Mix ingredients for topping and thickly cover potatoes. Bake at 400° for 15 minutes until tops are golden brown. (You may also want to run them under the broiler for 1 minute.) Serve halves on leaf lettuce or with a simple green salad.

Basil Shrimp Cakes

4 little meals

This dish is a good reason for growing basil in your window box! Less than a cup of fragrant leaves will give you a Little Meal for four, including the sauce. Use Italian arborio rice, fresh mozzarella and a good-quality Parmesan cheese. The simplicity of the dish makes high-quality ingredients essential. Fast and elegant.

2 qts. water

½ tbsp. salt

1⅓ cups arborio rice

6 oz. chopped cooked shrimp

5 plum tomatoes, seeded and chopped

¼ cup julienned basil leaves

6 oz. mozzarella cheese, diced

2 tbsp. butter

¾ cup freshly grated Parmesan cheese

Salt and pepper to taste

Fresh basil leaves

1. Bring water to a boil, add salt and rice. Cover pot and cook over moderate heat for 20 to 25 minutes until rice is tender.

2. Drain rice in colander and put into bowl. Add all ingredients and mix well.

3. Divide evenly onto plates and pack down into 1-inch-thick pancakes. Garnish with fresh basil leaves and serve with a cruet of olive oil.

4. Make pesto sauce (see below) and put a dollop on top. Or make Tomato-Basil Sauce (see page 183) and spoon around the perimeter.

Pesto Pronto

⅔ cup fresh basil leaves

1 clove garlic, quartered

2 tbsp. grated Parmesan cheese

1½ tbsp. olive oil

1. Place first 3 ingredients in food processor.

2. Blend and slowly add oil until sauce emulsifies.

Sausage Spoonbread in a Mug
4 little meals

This is an old-time Southern favorite. Use your biggest coffee mugs that you've filled to the brim with soft, creamy cornmeal and savory sausage. Glazed Delicious apples are this dish's best friend.

8 breakfast sausages, approx. ½ lb.

¾ cup cornmeal

2 cups water

3 eggs, beaten

1 cup buttermilk

⅓ cup grated Parmesan cheese

2 tbsp. finely minced scallions, white and green parts

2 tsp. sugar

1½ tsp. salt

Pinch cayenne pepper

Glazed apples (see page 180)

Mint sprigs

1. Preheat oven to 350°. Brown sausages in skillet or in broiler. Let cool and slice ¼-inch thick.

2. Put cornmeal in bowl with 1 cup water. Let sit 5 minutes.

3. In saucepan, heat remaining cup of water and add wet cornmeal and any excess water. Cook for 2 minutes, stirring constantly. Return cornmeal to bowl.

4. In separate bowl, mix eggs, buttermilk, cheese, scallions, sugar, salt and cayenne pepper. Add to cornmeal, mix well and add sliced sausages. Mixture will be loose.

5. Lightly oil 4 large ovenproof coffee mugs and divide mixture evenly into each. Place mugs on cookie sheet and bake 30 minutes.

6. Handles on mugs will be hot. Remove from oven with pot holders and let mugs rest 5 minutes before serving. When handles can be touched, the spoonbread is ready to eat. Serve with glazed apples and fresh mint.

Glazed Apples
2 red Delicious apples, unpeeled

3 tbsp. sugar

1. Cut each apple into 10 wedges. Remove seeds.

2. Cook apples and sugar over high heat in nonstick skillet until sugar begins to caramelize. Lower heat and turn apples so that they brown on each side. (Be careful not to overcook or they will taste bitter.)

3. Serve alongside spoonbread mugs.

Tian of Eggplant & Tomato, Goat Cheese Crouton

4 little meals

A *tian* is an earthenware ovenproof dish from Provence used to make all kinds of gratin dishes. This layered vegetable gratin is delicious hot, cold or in between. The longer you bake it the better it gets because its flavors intensify and texture firms up while you're off doing something else. Add a crouton spread with a fresh, local goat cheese.

1 large eggplant

½ tbsp. salt

4 medium onions

6 ripe tomatoes

1½ tbsp. dried basil leaves

1½ tsp. dried thyme leaves

2 tbsp. grated Parmesan cheese

½ cup fruity olive oil

Cheese Crouton:

4 long rectangular croutons, 5 by 2 by ¼ inch

6 oz. goat cheese

Fresh herb sprigs

1. Peel eggplant. Slice into thin rounds and sprinkle with salt. Put in colander and let drain 30 minutes.

2. Peel onions and slice very thin. Slice tomatoes very thin.

3. In 12- by 8-inch rectangular or oval baking dish, put layer of onions, top with layer of eggplant, then layer of tomatoes.

4. Sprinkle with 1 tbsp. basil and 1 tsp. thyme and repeat process. Make a final layer of thinly sliced onion. Sprinkle with Parmesan cheese and remaining basil and thyme.

5. Pour olive oil evenly over dish and bake at 300° for 3 hours. Once during baking, press down vegetables with a spatula.

6. Remove from oven and drain liquid. Serve hot, at room temperature or cold.

7. Make croutons from Italian bread. Toast lightly and spread with cheese. Garnish with fresh herbs.

Spaghetti Pudding, Tomato-Basil Sauce

6 to 8 little meals

This is for cheese lovers because it can be made with whatever varieties light up your taste buds: subtle Gruyère, pungent Pont-l'Évêque, blue cheese or the Fontina I've selected. Use as a Little Meal or as a surprise accompaniment to a small grilled steak.

¾ lb. spaghetti

4 eggs

1 cup ricotta cheese

¾ cup sour cream

1¾ cups milk

¾ cup shredded Fontina or Gruyère cheese

⅓ cup grated Parmesan cheese

1 clove garlic, pushed through garlic press

Salt and pepper

Tomato-Basil Sauce:

3 tbsp. olive oil

½ lb. red onion, finely chopped

28-oz. can Italian plum tomatoes

3 tbsp. tomato paste

2 tbsp. dried basil leaves

1 tsp. sugar

1 tsp. salt

Freshly ground black pepper

Topping:

¾ cup plain breadcrumbs

2 tbsp. butter, melted

2 tbsp. grated Parmesan cheese

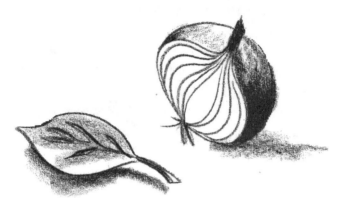

1. Cook spaghetti, drain and set aside.

2. In mixing bowl combine eggs, ricotta, sour cream, milk, cheeses, garlic, salt and pepper. Stir until smooth, then stir in spaghetti.

3. Cover and refrigerate overnight.

4. Heat oil in pot and add onion. Cook 5 minutes until soft.

5. Add remaining ingredients for sauce, cover pot and cook over moderate heat for 30 minutes. Let cool and refrigerate.

6. Next day preheat oven to 350°. Lightly grease 9- by 9-inch baking dish. Pour in pasta mixture. Make topping by mixing ingredients in small bowl and sprinkle on top.

7. Bake 50 minutes. Gently heat tomato-basil sauce and serve with large squares of spaghetti pudding.

Tortellini Gratinati

4 little meals

I created this dish for a well-known restaurant in New York in 1981. The restaurant has closed but the dish lives on. Use cheese-filled fresh tortellini, tricolored if possible, because the results are beautiful to look at and eat. *Buon appetito!*

⅓ cup heavy cream

2 tbsp. unsalted butter

6 oz. Gorgonzola cheese

¾ lb. tricolored cheese tortellini, cooked and drained

¼ cup heavy cream

⅓ cup grated Parmesan cheese

½ cup fresh breadcrumbs mixed with 1 tsp. olive oil

Fresh basil leaves

1. In heavy large skillet, put ⅓ cup heavy cream, butter and cheese.

2. Heat slowly until cheese melts and sauce has a smooth, creamy texture. Stir frequently with wooden spoon.

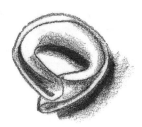

3. Add cooked tortellini, ¼ cup heavy cream, Parmesan cheese and toss well.

4. Divide pasta and sauce into 4 flat soup plates. Sprinkle each with 2 tbsp. breadcrumbs.

5. Put soup plates on baking sheet and put under broiler for 1 minute until breadcrumbs are lightly browned. Remove from oven.

6. Garnish with fresh basil leaves.

Palacsintas with Apricot Jam

4 little desserts

Hungarian cuisine, once considered the finest of Europe, is making a comeback! These delicate crepes are an old-world dessert filled with *lekvar* (apricot or prune butter) or the best-quality jam you can find. At the fabulously restored Gundel restaurant in Budapest, our friend George Lang serves it filled with walnuts and rum and topped with a warm chocolate sauce.

1 cup whole milk

1 cup plus 2 tbsp. flour

2 tbsp. sugar

2 eggs

Pinch salt

1 tbsp. melted butter

3 tbsp. cold butter

½ cup apricot jam

Powdered sugar

1. Preheat oven to 250°.

2. Blend milk, flour, sugar, eggs, salt and melted butter in food processor until smooth.

3. Melt 1 tsp. butter in 8-inch nonstick skillet until it sizzles. Coat bottom of pan with batter so that you have a very thin layer. Let crepe brown lightly and turn over. Cook 30 seconds.

4. While still in pan, put 1 tbsp. jam in a line down center of crepe and fold like a jelly roll, pressing down as you roll. Remove to baking sheet covered with foil and keep warm in oven until you have made 8.

5. Serve 2 per person on large plates. Sprinkle with powdered sugar.

Bon Temps Brûlée

4 little desserts

A combination of two fashionable desserts, this warm fruit gratin is made with zabaglione and looks like crème brûlée.

1 cup fresh blueberries	4 egg yolks
1½ cups fresh raspberries	2½ tbsp. sugar
	6 tbsp. marsala
	¼ cup dark brown sugar

1. Wash berries, drain well and mix; divide evenly into 4 small gratin dishes.

2. Beat the eggs and sugar in small bowl until they are pale-yellow and creamy.

3. Put mixture in top of double boiler over medium heat. Add marsala and continue to beat with wire whisk until very thick.

4. Spoon sauce over fruit to cover completely. Refrigerate.

5. Before serving, sprinkle gratins evenly with brown sugar. Broil until sugar melts and forms a crackling surface. Serve warm or at room temperature.

Chapter VIII

Little Meals with a Kick

All over the country, people are craving food that will light up their tastebuds! We've been smitten by salsa, which has replaced catsup as the favorite national condiment. We are demanding dishes that are colorful, tingling with acids of fruit and exotic vinegars and hot, hot, hot. It looks as if the chile pepper may become our national vegetable, as we've turned in our salt shakers for bottles of hot sauce on every table in America!

In the last two decades, a new flood of immigration has altered the way we eat in America, breaking a two-century tyranny of bland Eurocentric cooking. Our new multicultural national menu is packed with zippy ingredients from Mexico, the Caribbean, and Southeast Asia. They are defining a new cuisine for us, and we're happily going along for the culinary ride.

Not all the recipes in this chapter use chile peppers or Tabasco for their piquancy. Fresh ginger, scallions, garlic, cilantro, lime juice and vinegar will add verve to any dish and energize conversation around the dinner table.

I've steered clear of mysterious ingredients and simplified these recipes so that virtually every Little Meal can be prepared using products available in supermarkets, but you may find these products used in new ways, in combinations you've never thought of.

Caesar Salad with Roasted Red Pepper, Prosciutto Breadsticks
4 little meals

Caesar Cardini would be surprised to see what's happened to his salad since 1924. I've brightened it up with a roasted red pepper and turned it into a whole meal with prosciutto-wrapped breadsticks. As a bonus, the dressing has no egg.

2 large red peppers

8 thin slices prosciutto

8 long, thin breadsticks

Caesar Dressing:

½ cup olive oil

3 cloves garlic, pushed through garlic press

3 tbsp. fresh lemon juice

6 anchovy fillets, minced

1 tsp. Dijon mustard

1 tsp. Worcestershire sauce

Freshly ground black pepper

1 large head romaine, washed and cut into ¾-inch pieces

⅔ cup freshly grated Parmesan cheese

1 cup croutons, homemade if possible (see **Note**)

1. Hold whole peppers over an open flame or place in broiler until they get very black, about 10 minutes. Put in paper bag to steam. Peel skins, cut peppers in half lengthwise and remove seeds.

2. Wrap prosciutto, spiral-fashion, around breadsticks. Reserve.

3. Whisk together ingredients for dressing.

4. In large bowl, put lettuce and cheese. Add dressing and mix thoroughly. Add croutons and mix again.

5. Divide salad evenly onto chilled plates. Top each with a red pepper half and 2 breadsticks on the side.

Note: I like to make rye croutons: Cut 2 pieces of rye bread into cubes and sauté in 1½ tbsp. olive oil.

Lime-Chicken Brochettes with Guacamole & Tortilla Ribbons

4 little meals

Now you know the way to Santa Fe! I love the contrasts of smooth guacamole, crisp tortillas and lime-infused chicken (you can substitute shrimp or pork). Follow this with Espresso Bean Chili (see page 200) and turn a Little Meal into a Southwest feast.

8 6-inch bamboo skewers

🪶

¾ lb. chicken breasts, skinless and boneless, cut into 1-inch cubes (32 pieces)

2 tbsp. fresh lime juice

2 tbsp. vegetable oil

1 clove garlic, pushed through garlic press

¼ tsp. salt

Tortilla Ribbons:

3 corn tortillas

1 tbsp. vegetable oil

Guacamole:

2 very ripe avocados, peeled and mashed

1 jalapeño pepper, seeded and minced

Juice of 1 lime

1 medium tomato, seeded and diced

2 tbsp. chopped scallions

2 tbsp. chopped cilantro

Salt and cayenne pepper to taste

🪶

4 lime wedges

194

1. Soak skewers in water for 30 minutes.

2. Thread 4 pieces of chicken on each skewer and put in shallow dish. Mix lime juice, oil, garlic and salt and pour over chicken. Let sit 30 minutes.

3. Cut tortillas into 1/16-inch-wide ribbons. In nonstick skillet heat oil and fry ribbons until crisp. Drain and set aside.

4. In medium bowl, mix all ingredients for guacamole. Refrigerate while you cook the chicken.

5. Remove skewers from marinade. Pat dry. Broil 2 minutes on each side until chicken is cooked but still juicy.

6. Evenly divide tortilla ribbons onto 4 plates. Top each portion with 2 chicken skewers, guacamole and a lime wedge.

Skewers of Shrimp & Cajun Sausage, Creole Rice

4 little meals

These are jambalaya flavors cooked in two parts so that you can savor them separately, then together. If you can't find real andouille (Cajun) sausage, substitute pepperoni or kielbasa or even hot Italian sausage. And don't forget the beer!

8 6-inch wooden skewers

Creole Rice:

2 tbsp. fruity olive oil

1 cup coarsely chopped onion

¾ cup chopped green bell pepper

1 cup long-grain rice

2 cups canned crushed tomatoes

1 tbsp. red wine vinegar

½ tsp. thyme leaves

1 tbsp. olive oil

16 jumbo shrimp, shelled

6 oz. andouille sausage, cut into 16 ½-inch-thick circles

¼ cup olive oil

Lime wedges

Hot sauce

1. Soak skewers in water for 30 minutes.

2. To make creole rice: Heat oil in skillet, then sauté onion, green pepper and rice until rice is slightly brown.

3. Add tomatoes, vinegar and thyme and cover. Simmer about 20 minutes until liquid is absorbed. Stir in 1 tbsp. olive oil. Keep warm.

4. Preheat broiler. Alternate 2 shrimp and 2 pieces of sausage on each skewer. Place 8 skewers on baking sheet and brush with olive oil. Broil on each side for 1 minute.

5. To assemble: Put a mound of creole rice on each of 4 plates. Put 2 skewers, overlapping at top, on rice. Serve with lime wedges and hot sauce, if desired.

Barbecued Salmon Brochettes, Pineapple Rice
4 little meals

This dish reminds me of Madame Butterfly and orange blossoms. It is a stunning Little Meal for company, accompanied by glasses of sake on ice with an unexpected twist of cucumber. Looks terrific on a black lacquered tray.

8 6-inch wooden skewers

¾ lb. salmon, cut into 32 1-inch chunks

1½ tbsp. soy sauce

¾ tbsp. honey

¾ tbsp. catsup

Pineapple Rice:

2 cups water

1 cup long-grain white rice

1 tbsp. minced fresh ginger

1 clove fresh garlic, minced

¼ tsp. salt

½ tbsp. sesame oil

½ tbsp. soy sauce

¾ cup chopped fresh pineapple

2 tbsp. minced scallions, green part

1. Soak skewers in water for 30 minutes.

2. Thread 4 pieces of salmon on each skewer. Put in shallow dish.

3. Mix soy sauce, honey and catsup. Pour over salmon. Let marinate ½ hour, turning skewers several times.

4. To make pineapple rice: In medium pot, boil water. Add rice, ginger, garlic and salt. Cover, lower heat and cook 20 minutes or until water is absorbed. Add sesame oil, soy sauce and pineapple. Mix well and keep warm.

5. Remove salmon brochettes from marinade. Broil or grill 2 to 3 minutes, keeping the inside rare.

6. To serve: Mound pineapple rice on 4 large plates. Top each portion with 2 salmon brochettes and sprinkle with minced scallions.

Espresso Bean Chili

6 to 8 little meals

Coffee is my favorite food. Little black turtle beans remind me of coffee beans and also gave me the inspiration to add espresso to this aromatic vegetarian chili. Dark and mysterious: That's how I like it.

½ lb. black beans, soaked overnight

1 large bay leaf

¼ cup vegetable oil

4 cloves fresh garlic, minced

3 cups chopped onions

1½ tbsp. instant espresso

1½ tbsp. chile powder

1 tbsp. ground cumin

1 tbsp. oregano leaves

1 tsp. salt

2¾ cups canned crushed tomatoes

🖋

½ cup crème fraîche

1. Drain beans. Put in large heavy pot with bay leaf. Cover with 2 inches of water. Bring to simmer.

2. Put oil in medium pot. Add garlic and onions and cook 10 minutes until soft but not brown.

3. Add espresso, chile powder, cumin, oregano and salt. Cook 5 minutes over low heat, stirring often.

4. Add crushed tomatoes and cook 15 minutes.

5. Add to beans and mix well. Make sure beans are covered by 1 inch of liquid. If not, add water.

6. Cover and cook over low heat for 2 hours. Uncover and cook another ½ hour until chili is thick and beans are tender.

7. Serve chili in large, flat soup plates. Spoon 1 to 2 tbsp. crème fraîche in center of each.

8. Serve with little bowls of chopped coriander, shredded Monterey Jack cheese, chopped scallions, shaved bitter chocolate, sliced jalapeños and hot wheat tortillas.

Crème Fraîche

1 cup

1 cup heavy cream, at room temperature
3 tbsp. buttermilk

1. Put cream and buttermilk in warm jar with cover.

2. Leave at room temperature for 12 to 24 hours until it thickens. Refrigerate. Keeps for 1 week.

White Polenta & Black Bean Chili

4 little meals

The secret to this dish is to make too much Espresso Bean Chili, because the white polenta is so easy to make and turns the surplus into a brand-new experience! You'll adore the contrasts of color and taste.

Polenta:

5 cups water

½ tbsp. salt

1 ½ cups white cornmeal

2 cups Espresso Bean Chili (see page 200)

Fresh cilantro leaves

1. Bring water and salt to a boil in a heavy medium pot.

2. Add cornmeal very slowly, stirring constantly to make sure it is smooth. Continue to cook 20 to 25 minutes until thick.

3. Heat chili in small saucepan until very hot.

4. Spread cooked cornmeal evenly on 4 plates. Make a well in the center of each and spoon into it ½ cup chili. Garnish with lots of cilantro leaves.

Lobster & Banana Calypso
4 little meals

What else can you call such a salad whose dressing is spiked with dark Caribbean rum? Rum-soaked, sun-dried cranberries are an improvisation that add even more color and flavor. Serve with lots of lime wedges and a basket of warm plantain chips.

¼ cup sun-dried cranberries

¼ cup dark rum

¼ cup hot water

¾ cup mayonnaise

1½ tbsp. dark rum

3 tbsp. catsup

½ tsp. hot sauce

1 lb. cooked lobster meat

2 large, ripe bananas

Mâche or arugula

1. Soak sun-dried cranberries in rum and water for 30 minutes.

2. Mix mayonnaise, rum, catsup and hot sauce in small bowl. Chill 30 minutes.

3. Cut lobster into 1-inch chunks. Slice bananas ½ inch thick. Mix together in bowl.

4. Put mâche or arugula on 4 plates. Top with lobster and bananas.

5. Cover each portion with ¼ cup dressing. Drain cranberries and scatter over tops of salads.

Olé *Mole* in Flour Tortillas

4 little meals

A real *mole* is a complicated sauce. This version is easy and has, of course, unsweetened chocolate as its signature ingredient, plus a soupçon of coffee liqueur. I've made it here with turkey, as tradition dictates, but it's also a saucy medium for leftover chicken.

Mole Sauce:

2 tbsp. lard or oil

2 medium onions, chopped

2 cloves garlic, minced

3 tbsp. raisins

¼ tsp. cinnamon

¼ tsp. anise seed

½ tsp. ground cumin

¼ tsp. ground allspice

1½ tbsp. chile powder

1 tbsp. toasted sesame seeds

1 oz. tortilla chips, in pieces

1 tbsp. mild canned green chiles, chopped

2 tomatoes, chopped

½ tsp. salt

2 tbsp. coffee liqueur

2 cups chicken stock

½ oz. unsweetened chocolate, grated

1¼ lbs. turkey cutlets, poached or grilled

16 small flour tortillas

½ cup each: chopped scallions, chopped cilantro, sour cream

1. In large pot, heat lard or oil. Add chopped onions and garlic and sauté 10 minutes until soft but not browned.

2. Add rest of ingredients for sauce *except* ½ cup chicken stock and chocolate. Stir well and cook 3 minutes, then put contents of pot into food processor.

3. Process until very smooth, approximately 2 minutes.

4. Pour puréed ingredients back into pot. Add remaining chicken stock. Mix well.

5. Cook over medium heat for 45 minutes, stirring frequently. Add grated chocolate and cook 5 minutes.

6. Cut turkey into ⅓-inch julienne. Add to sauce and warm thoroughly.

7. On small flour tortilla, put turkey and *mole* sauce. Add chopped scallions, cilantro and sour cream, if desired. Roll up. Place several on each plate and top with spoonfuls of sauce.

Chicken "Godonov," Kidney Bean & Walnut Salad

4 little meals

In Brooklyn's Brighton Beach, Primorski Restaurant is an out-of-century experience where the language and cuisine are strictly Russian. I've topped their *lobio,* an authentic kidney bean and walnut salad, with skewers of garlic chicken, but you can also use shish kebob. Great with pepper or Horseradish Vodka (see opposite)! *Na Zdorovie!*

1 lb. skinless, boneless chicken breasts

Marinade:

¼ cup fresh lemon juice

¼ cup olive oil

2 cloves fresh garlic, minced

1 small onion, thinly sliced

2 bay leaves

2 cups cooked kidney beans (or canned)

2 tbsp. chopped red onion

⅓ cup walnuts, ground in food processor

¼ cup chopped cilantro

2 tbsp. red wine vinegar

2 tbsp. olive oil

Salt and cayenne pepper to taste

8 6-inch wooden skewers

1. Cut chicken into 1-inch cubes. Put in bowl and add ingredients for marinade. Cover and refrigerate. Let marinate 1 to 2 hours.

2. In medium bowl, mix remaining ingredients. Cover and refrigerate.

3. Soak skewers in water for 30 minutes.

4. Thread chicken on 8 6-inch skewers, putting 5 pieces on each. Pat dry and grill or broil until done but still juicy.

5. Heat marinade to boiling. Mound kidney bean salad evenly in center of plates. Top each with 2 skewers and drizzle 1 tbsp. of marinade over chicken.

Horseradish Vodka

1 small horseradish

1 bottle vodka

1. Peel horseradish. Cut several long, thin strips.

2. Add to vodka and infuse for 8 hours. Chill well and strain before serving.

Gazpacho Mary with Cheese Toast

4 little meals

We all know Bloody Mary, but do you know her Spanish cousin, Gazpacho? Another sort of crowd pleaser, gazpacho is a cold vegetable soup puréed to a thick, chewable liquid. Serve in a large wine glass and garnish as you would a Bloody Mary, with celery sticks and lime. Accompany with Cheese Toast (see opposite) and a jigger of pepper vodka.

1 carrot, peeled

½ green pepper, seeded

½ red pepper, seeded

3 scallions

1 cucumber, peeled and seeded

28 oz. canned tomatoes in purée

2 tbsp. red wine vinegar

2 tbsp. olive oil

1 tbsp. hot sauce

¼ tsp. ground allspice

Salt to taste

3 to 4 tbsp. chilled pepper vodka

4 celery sticks

4 lime slices

1. Cut all fresh vegetables into 1-inch pieces. Put in food processor with tomatoes and process until almost smooth.

2. Empty into bowl and add vinegar, olive oil, hot sauce, allspice and salt. Stir well and chill.

3. To serve: Add desired amount of vodka and mix well. Divide soup evenly into large, chilled wine glasses. Garnish with celery sticks and lime slices. Serve with Cheese Toast right from the oven.

Cheese Toast

1 egg

3 oz. cream cheese, softened

5 tbsp. shredded Gruyère cheese

¼ tsp. hot sauce

4 slices firm white bread, crusts removed

1. Preheat oven to 425°.

2. In small bowl mix egg, cream cheese, Gruyère and hot sauce. Blend until smooth.

3. Spread evenly on bread and place on baking sheet.

4. Bake for 15 minutes until golden brown.

Chicken Muffaletta

4 little meals

This enormous sandwich is the trademark of the Central Grocery in New Orleans. Its famous olive salad is usually heaped on layers of deli meats and provolone. I think it's even more delicious on a warm, succulent chili-rubbed breast of chicken, grilled to perfection. Sure to become a family favorite. Sazerac, anyone?

Olive Salad:

1 cup green olives with pimientos, chopped

1 large clove garlic, minced

2 anchovy fillets, minced

1 tbsp. capers

⅓ cup finely chopped celery

⅓ cup chopped fresh parsley

1 tsp. dried oregano leaves

½ cup fruity olive oil

Freshly ground black pepper

4 4-oz. skinless, boneless chicken breasts

1 tbsp. chile powder

1 tsp. salt

4 kaiser rolls, split and toasted

Leaf lettuce

1. Mix all ingredients for olive salad in bowl. Cover and refrigerate.

2. Dust chicken on both sides with chile powder and salt. Broil 2 to 3 minutes on each side until done but juicy.

3. Put leaf lettuce on bottom half of each roll. Top with a warm chicken breast and lots of olive salad.

4. Cut sandwich in half. Serve with carrot sticks and Cajun potato chips.

Thunder & Lightning

(orecchiette with fried chick-peas & pepper)

4 little meals

A chef in Hoboken, New Jersey, translated this recipe from an old Italian cookbook. Thunder refers to the profusion of fried chick-peas, and lightning to the excessive amount of cracked black pepper. (All are tossed with pasta, chicken broth, cheese and sage.) Did you know there are more than six hundred pasta shapes in the world? I like to use orecchiette (little ears), but you can use bow ties, as the chef does.

3 qts. water

¾ lb. orecchiette pasta

½ tbsp. salt

¼ cup olive oil

2 cloves garlic, minced

2 cups cooked chick-peas
(15½-oz. can, drained)

1 tsp. dried sage leaves

1 cup chicken broth

1½ tsp. cracked pepper, Italian-style, or mignonette

2 tbsp. butter

Salt to taste

½ cup grated Parmesan cheese

1. Bring water to a boil. Add pasta and salt. Cook al dente.

2. In nonstick skillet heat olive oil. Add garlic and chick-peas and cook over high heat until chick-peas begin to pop.

3. Add sage, broth and pepper. Lower heat and let broth reduce by a quarter.

4. Drain pasta well. Put in large bowl with butter. Add chick-peas and broth and toss well.

5. Add salt to taste and half the cheese. Divide evenly into warm bowls and serve with remaining cheese.

Goombay Chicken & Baked Pineapple

4 little meals

This hot bird is made in the style of jerk chicken, the signature dish of Jamaica, aggressively seasoned and meltingly tender. You can make it with Scotch bonnet peppers as tradition dictates, but they're hard to find and hot to handle! Instead, use as much Tabasco sauce and black pepper as your taste buds allow. Tabasco-laced pineapple is a definite new taste sensation. Bake this or grill it outdoors. Shake up a pitcher of goombay cocktails (see opposite).

4 chicken thighs

4 chicken drumsticks

¾ cup finely chopped onions

½ cup white vinegar

¼ cup olive oil

¼ cup orange juice

3 tbsp. lime juice

1 tbsp. sugar

1 tbsp. salt

1 tbsp. dried thyme leaves

1½ tbsp. ground allspice

3 cloves garlic, pushed through garlic press

2 tsp. Tabasco sauce

Freshly ground black pepper

4 ¾-inch-thick slices peeled fresh pineapple, cut in half

1. Put all ingredients in large bowl. Cover and refrigerate. Marinate for 3 hours or longer.

2. Preheat oven to 375°.

3. Remove chicken and pineapple from marinade, put in baking pan and bake for 50 minutes.

4. In small saucepan reduce marinade by half.

5. Serve 2 pieces of pineapple, 1 leg and 1 thigh on each plate, and spoon marinade on top. Serve with goombay cocktails.

Goombay Cocktail
4 cocktails

½ cup light rum

½ cup dark rum

1 cup pineapple juice

2 tbsp. lime juice

¼ cup cream of coconut, sweetened

Shake all ingredients with ice in cocktail shaker until frothy. Strain over ice cubes in big, festive glasses.

Red Bean Hash, Poached Egg & Salsa
2 little meals

Red beans mashed with hot sauce and cornmeal look just like corned beef hash. These patties fry up crispy on the outside and creamy on the inside. A Little Meal to get you going any time of the day.

1 ¾ cups cooked kidney beans (or 15½-oz. can, drained)

1 egg

1 tsp. cumin

2 tsp. hot sauce

¼ cup cornmeal

½ tsp. salt

1 ½ tbsp. vegetable oil

2 eggs

½ cup prepared salsa

Fresh cilantro leaves

1. Put beans in food processor and blend 30 seconds. Add egg, cumin, hot sauce, cornmeal and salt and process until they form a thick paste. Refrigerate ½ hour or longer.

2. Heat oil in nonstick skillet. Form bean paste into 2 thick patties. Fry on each side 2 to 3 minutes until brown and crusty.

3. Poach 2 eggs or fry sunny side up.

4. To serve: Put red bean hash in center of each plate. Top with an egg and surround hash with a circle of salsa. Garnish with cilantro.

"Hot Lips" BBQ Mussels, Zwieback
2 little meals

Because they're served out of the shell, I make this dish only when mammoth mussels are available and there are twelve or fewer to the pound. Peppery, hot and juicy, they plump up in a piquant sauce of dry vermouth and Worcestershire. You'll lick the plate clean.

4 tbsp. butter

⅔ cup chopped onion

1 cup dry vermouth

3 tsp. cracked black pepper

¼ tsp. cayenne pepper

½ tsp. dried rosemary leaves

½ tsp. oregano leaves

2 tsp. Worcestershire sauce

2 lbs. large mussels, scrubbed and debearded

4 slices zwieback (see page 101) or French bread, toasted on both sides

½ cup dry vermouth

½ tsp. salt

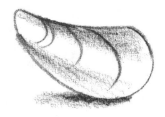

1. Melt butter in large pot and sauté onions until soft but not brown.

2. Add 1 cup vermouth, black pepper, cayenne, herbs and Worcestershire sauce. Bring to a boil and add mussels. Cover and shake pot back and forth until mussels open, about 10 minutes.

3. Remove mussels from pot with a slotted spoon. Discard any that do not open. Take mussels out of shells and place on warm plates with 2 slices of toast alongside each.

4. Add ½ cup vermouth and salt to pot and reduce sauce quickly until it has thickened slightly. Pour sauce over mussels and zwieback.

Barbecued Onion & Chicken Quesadilla

4 little meals

Here's a Tex-Mex way to turn leftover chicken (or turkey) into a whole new dish, smothered in barbecued onions and smoky cheese, then layered between crisp tortillas. Wash down with tequila-spiked lemonade for an unforgettable experience.

¾ lb. onions, peeled and sliced thin

1 tsp. oil

½ cup barbecue sauce (your favorite)

12 6-inch flour tortillas

¼ cup chopped cilantro

¼ cup minced scallions

¾ lb. grilled, poached or baked chicken, skinless and boneless (cut into small strips)

1 large red pepper, seeded and thinly sliced

¾ lb. shredded cheese, Monterey Jack and smoked mozzarella

Shredded lettuce

Sour cream or plain yogurt

1. Cook onions in nonstick skillet in oil for 5 minutes until they soften. Add barbecue sauce and cook over low heat for 10 minutes more.

2. Preheat oven to 425°.

3. Layer each quesadilla bottom-up as follows:

> tortilla
>
> barbecued onions to cover
>
> 1½ oz. cheese
>
> 1 tbsp. cilantro
>
> 1 tbsp. scallions
>
> second tortilla
>
> 3 oz. chicken pieces
>
> 4 slices red pepper
>
> 1½ oz. cheese
>
> third tortilla

Brush top lightly with oil.

4. Put on baking sheet and bake for 8 to 10 minutes until top is lightly browned.

5. Put 1 quesadilla on each plate. Cut in quarters. Place shredded lettuce in center and top with sour cream or yogurt.

Silver-Dollar Crabcakes, Tomato-Corn Relish
4 little meals

Bet you can't eat just one! Succulent little mounds of crab top a refreshing tomato relish tossed with bits of lemon and corn. The silver-dollar size makes these crabcakes luxurious hors d'oeuvres.

Extra, extra: For a deluxe little meal, make the crabcakes hamburger-size and put them in a puddle of leftover gazpacho (see page 208)!

1 lb. jumbo lump crabmeat

1 egg yolk

½ cup mayonnaise

½ tbsp. dry mustard

1 tsp. Worcestershire sauce

½ tsp. hot sauce

2 tbsp. minced fresh herbs (parsley, basil, cilantro, tarragon)

1 cup unseasoned breadcrumbs

½ cup vegetable oil

Tomato-Corn Relish:

¾ lb. plum tomatoes, seeded and finely diced

1 tbsp. minced shallots

⅓ cup cooked corn kernels

Pulp of 1 lemon, chopped

1 tbsp. minced fresh cilantro

1 tbsp. fruity olive oil

1. In large bowl mix all ingredients for crabcakes except bread-crumbs and oil.

2. Scoop out 24 balls and roll in breadcrumbs. Coat evenly, making little crabcakes the size of silver dollars. Refrigerate until ready to use.

3. Mix ingredients for tomato-corn relish and refrigerate.

4. Heat oil in large pan to 375°. Add crabcakes and fry on both sides until brown.

5. Put tomato-corn relish in center of each plate and surround with 6 crabcakes.

New Orleans Shrimp & Chicken Creole, Cornbread Toast

4 little meals

Put your favorite Louis Armstrong tunes in the CD player and let these seductive aromas fill your kitchen. If you don't want to make your own cornbread, try some day-old corn muffins and toast them gently. A great low-fat one-pot dish.

½ cup chicken stock

½ cup red pepper, in ¼-inch dice

½ cup green pepper, in ¼-inch dice

1 cup finely chopped scallions

½ cup finely chopped celery

3 cloves fresh garlic, minced

2 cups canned crushed tomatoes

½ cup dry red wine

2 tbsp. tomato paste

2 tbsp. red wine vinegar

½ tsp. thyme leaves

¼ tsp. mace

¼ tsp. allspice

1 tsp. chile powder

1 bay leaf

¼ tsp. salt

1 cup fresh okra, cut into ½-inch pieces

½ lb. chicken breasts, cut into ½-inch julienne strips

3 oz. pepperoni, cut into ⅛-inch-thick slices

½ lb. medium shrimp, peeled

4 large corn muffins, split and toasted

1. Heat stock in large enameled pan over medium heat.

2. Add peppers, scallions, celery and garlic and cook for 10 minutes.

3. Add tomatoes, wine, tomato paste, vinegar, herbs and spices. Bring to a boil, lower heat and simmer 10 minutes.

4. Add okra and cook 5 minutes.

5. Add chicken breasts and heat until chicken is cooked.

6. Add pepperoni and shrimp and cook 3 minutes until shrimp are done.

7. To serve: Put 2 halves of corn muffin on each plate, toasted side up. Cover with 1½ cups of shrimp and chicken creole.

Spicy Thai Chicken with Red Peppers & Peanuts
4 little meals

This dish is best when made in a wok so that the individual ingredients cook quickly. Ginger, garlic, lemon and scallions give an authentic flavor. You control the "heat" with red pepper flakes. Top with a pile of chow mein noodles and eat with chopsticks.

2 tbsp. corn oil

1 lb. skinless, boneless chicken breasts, cut into 1-inch pieces

1 tbsp. fresh ginger, finely minced

2 cloves garlic, minced

2 medium-sized red peppers

½ lb. fresh spinach

4 scallions, cut into 1½-inch diagonal pieces

⅓ cup fresh cilantro, chopped

½ tsp. red pepper flakes

⅓ cup unsalted peanuts

¾ cup chicken stock

1 tbsp. soy sauce

1 tbsp. fresh lemon juice

1½ tsp. arrowroot, dissolved in a little water

1 cup chow mein noodles

1. Heat oil in large skillet or wok. Sauté chicken pieces until just cooked through, stirring often. With slotted spoon remove chicken to bowl.

2. Add minced ginger and garlic to pan. Cook 2 minutes.

3. Cut red peppers in half lengthwise and remove seeds. Cut into ½-inch-thick slices horizontally. Add to pan and sauté 3 to 4 minutes.

4. Add spinach, scallions, cilantro, red pepper flakes and peanuts. Cook 2 to 3 minutes. With slotted spoon remove ingredients to bowl with chicken.

5. To remaining juices in pan, add chicken stock, soy sauce and lemon juice and bring to a boil. Add arrowroot and whisk until sauce thickens.

6. Add chicken and vegetables to sauce and cook over high heat 1 minute. Divide evenly onto 4 plates.

7. Top with chow mein noodles.

Candied Ginger Cake, Vanilla Ice Cream
8 little desserts

This simple cake has a snappy, intriguing flavor from lots of chopped candied ginger. It's butter-rich and delicious served warm with vanilla ice cream.

1 cup butter, at room temperature

1 cup sugar

2 cups flour, sifted

1 egg, beaten

½ tsp. salt

6 tbsp. finely chopped candied ginger

1 pt. vanilla ice cream

1. Preheat oven to 350°.

2. Cream together butter and sugar. Add flour and half of beaten egg. Add salt and ginger.

3. Press into 8-inch pie plate. Brush top with remaining half of egg and score in a crisscross pattern with the back of a knife.

4. Bake for 30 minutes. Let cool 15 minutes. Serve each portion with a small scoop of ice cream.

Drunken Fruit Compote

4 little desserts

Even though compote, a kind of Slavic fruit stew, is a popular winter dessert, I like to serve it all year long, adding seasonal berries depending on the month. Fresh raspberries and blackberries are my favorites. And since no one's smoking these days, why not serve with sweet rolled cigars you can eat (see opposite)!

11 oz. mixed dried fruit

2 oz. black raisins

2 oz. gold raisins

2 cups water

2 oz. whole peeled almonds

1 sliced lemon

¼ cup sugar

2 cups water

2 cinnamon sticks, broken in half

½ cup dry sherry

½ cup fresh orange juice

1 cup fresh raspberries or blackberries (optional)

1. Bring all fruits and 2 cups water to a boil.

2. Reduce heat, add almonds, lemon, sugar and 2 more cups of water. Simmer 10 minutes. Remove from heat.

3. Put in large bowl. Add cinnamon sticks, sherry and orange juice. Add fresh berries, if using.

4. Chill well. This is better the next day.

Cinnamon-Sugar Cigars
12 pieces

12 phyllo sheets

1/2 stick unsalted butter, melted

3 tbsp. sugar mixed with 1/2 tbsp. ground cinnamon

1. Preheat oven to 350°.

2. Cut large sheets of phyllo in half.

3. Brush 2 phyllo half-sheets with butter, roll up like a cigar and brush the outside with melted butter. Sprinkle generously with cinnamon-sugar.

4. Place on baking sheet. Repeat process until you make 12 cigars. Bake for 10 minutes. Let cool.

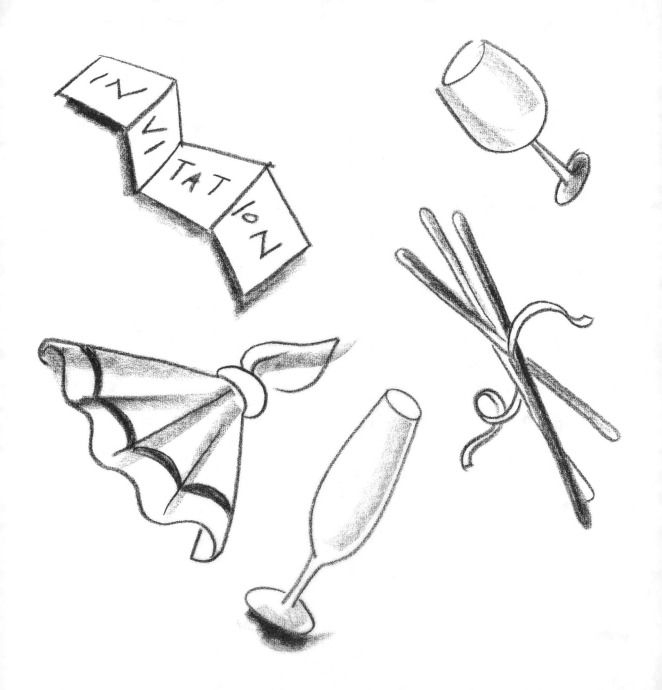

Chapter IX

Entertaining with Little Meals

Entertaining is as much a state of mind as it is a way to communicate. We please ourselves when we give pleasure, especially when food is the medium. Imagine, every time we feed someone else we give both physical and emotional sustenance! And, perhaps, a good time.

These days entertaining demands style and surprise, even when the guests are your family. Because we've outgrown huge bowls of soggy pasta and pasty tuna fish salad, the essence of this book is to delight guests with a parade of Little Meals, each plated in its own definitive style, each succeeded by another as theme, taste, temperature or your own good instincts dictate.

There are no strict categories of appetizers, main courses or salads in this book, nor are there specific mealtimes. Instead, you can organize a memorable meal by creatively mixing and matching dishes, morning, noon and night.

The wonder of Little Meals is that when served together, they make elegant little menus for entertaining family or friends. The secret is to choose two or more recipes that reflect a theme or sentiment. Use your table as a stage, and set it with imagination and flair.

Entertaining Tips for Little or No Money

1. Tie long, thin breadsticks with ribbons.

2. Use beautiful lacquered chopsticks for all dishes with Oriental flavors.

3. Create your own "condiment bar" on a tray that's passed around the table.

4. Instead of napkins, put large linen dish towels in napkin rings.

5. Use large plates, ten to twelve inches, when serving one Little Meal; use eight-inch plates when serving a succession of Little Meals.

6. Use different plate patterns for every course.

7. Create your own wine tasting: Give every two guests their own bottle of wine. Encourage sharing.

8. Make place cards with funny sayings.

9. Have each guest bring a homemade dessert: This saves time and money and is fun for all.

10. Make something extra to give to your guests as they leave: cookies, candies or spiced nuts wrapped beautifully.

11. Serve hors d'oeuvres and drinks in the kitchen.

12. If you have a very large kitchen, give everyone a task to do. You supply the aprons.

13. Make an edible centerpiece and draw numbers for it at the end of the meal.

14. Serve finger bowls with lemon slices and cardamom seeds between courses.

15. Steam little white washcloths, rolled up, in your vegetable steamer and pass around after the meal.

16. Mix up a pitcher of "Arnold Palmers" for your friends who don't drink—half fresh lemonade/half iced tea.

17. Create a "coffee bar": Serve hot coffee accompanied by a tray with small bowls of shaved chocolate, whipped cream, cinnamon sticks, vanilla sugar, lump sugar and several liqueurs.

18. Make two dramatically different desserts and serve alternately to guests. This encourages sharing and conversation.

19. Collect wrapped sugar cubes from your trips all over the world. Serve in a crystal bowl with hot drinks.

20. If your guests enjoyed a particular dish, calligraph the recipe and send it to everyone who was there.

Unexpected Guests

I always have eight different kinds of pasta and beans on hand for unexpected dinners. I can do anything with them. And I always have pounds of nuts: Toasted in a hot oven with some fresh herbs, they make excellent cocktail snacks. I can put them together when I hear guests at the door, and they're ready before my company sits down. I have baguettes in the freezer: Sliced thin and toasted, they're better than crackers. A can of Italian-style tuna whipped up with some olive oil and garlic and put into a pretty French ramekin makes a great pâté. We keep a big jar of olive oil in the kitchen and keep adding olives to it. The olives are perfect for cocktails, and the oil is intensified for cooking.

Entertaining Morning, Noon & Night

Little Meals can be served any time of the day. Here are ideas for breakfast, lunch and dinner and all those mealtimes in between.

Morning Little Meals
Breakfast:

Autumn Breakfast

Barcelona Bread

Tennessee Doughnuts & Ham Steak

Fried Green Tomatoes, Rosemary Mayonnaise

Red Bean Hash, Poached Egg & Salsa

Leftover Spaghetti Pudding, Tomato-Basil Sauce

Poached Eggs Piperade

"Green Eggs 'n' Ham"

Sausage Spoonbread in a Mug

Brunch:

Crab Dewey Shortcake

Lobster & Banana Calypso

St. Tropez Tart

Gazpacho Mary with Cheese Toast

BLT Quesadilla, Triple-Decker

Smoked Salmon Boboli

New Orleans Shrimp & Chicken Creole, Cornbread Toast

King Crab, Grapefruit & Avocado Salad, Chile-Lime Dressing

Smoked Salmon & Cucumber Linguine

235

Noon Little Meals
Lunch:
Espresso Bean Chili
Cherry Tomato Boboli
Poached Salmon with Cucumber-Mint Frappé
Baked Goat Cheese with Lima Beans & Bacon
Artichoke Antipasto in a Tuscan Bread
Cumin Chicken on Pita Bread Salad
"Mange-tout" Sesame Noodles
RRBBLT
Barbecued Onion & Chicken Quesadilla
Chicken Muffaletta
Basil Shrimp Cakes
Pasta Rustica
Sweet Pea Tortellini Salad

Afternoon:
Two Iced Fruit Soups, Cinnamon Toast
A Little Afternoon Tea
Tian of Eggplant & Tomato, Goat Cheese Crouton
Pork Honey Buns, Chinese-style
Japanese Custard in a Whole Red Pepper
Breadspreads
Goat Cheese & Lemon Curd, Fresh Raspberries
Sweet Baked Tomato
Blueberry Lemon-Buttermilk Shortcakes

Drunken Fruit Compote, Cinnamon-Sugar Cigars
Palacsintas with Apricot Jam
Napoleon with Gorgonzola, Pears & Walnuts

Night Little Meals
Hors d'oeuvres:

Do-It-Yourself Guacamole Kit
Warm Walnut Hummus, Chilled Vegetable Salad
"Hot Lips" BBQ Mussels, Zwieback
Seafood Quesadilla, Triple-Decker
Rosemary-Lemon Chicken Wings
Lime-Chicken Brochettes with Guacamole & Tortilla Ribbons
Skewers of Shrimp & Cajun Sausage, Creole Rice
Grilled Chorizos, Jicama-Orange Salad
Barbecued Salmon Brochettes, Pineapple Rice

Pretheater:

Seviche, Straight Up, with a Twist
Curried Ginger Chicken, Poppadum Crisp
Tortellini Gratinati
Mexican Corn & Rice Salad, Jumbo Shrimp
White Polenta & Black Bean Chili
Seared Salmon on a Moroccan Salad
Steamed Shrimp & Artichoke, Mustard Seed Dressing
Chicken "Godonov," Kidney Bean & Walnut Salad

Dinner:

Scallops Provençale on Olive Toast
Spicy Thai Chicken with Red Peppers & Peanuts
Cupid's Meatloaf, Tomato Glaze & Onion Arrows
Philippine Vinegar Chicken
Lemon Pasta with Asparagus
Sausage, Pepper & Olive Ragout
Chardonnay Chicken & Grapes on Minted Rice
A Little Chicken & Garlic Stew
Goombay Chicken & Baked Pineapple
Orzo "Risotto" with Wild Mushrooms
Mussels from Brussels
Spaghetti Pudding, Tomato-Basil Sauce
Thunder & Lightning
Orange-Ginger Lamb Riblets

Supper:

Silver-Dollar Crabcakes, Tomato-Corn Relish
"Couch Potatoes"
Gorgonzola & Polenta Melt, Arugula Julienne
Cabbage & Noodles
Filet Mignonettes, Celery Sticks & Blue Cheese Dressing
Caesar Salad with Roasted Red Pepper, Prosciutto Breadsticks
Swordfish Skewered on Rosemary Branches
Carpaccio Gold
Chicken Rollmops in Watercress Nests

Pastina in Garlic Broth
Pan-Seared Foie Gras, Sun-Dried Cranberry Sauce

Midnight Snack:
Jumbo Shrimp Cocktail "On the Rocks"
Cake of Steak Tartare "Iced" with Black Caviar
Salmagundi
Ultralight Chocolate Cake
Musician's Dessert

Cherry Tomato
Boboli

Cupid's Meatloaf
Tomato Glaze
Onion Arrows

Sweet Baked
Tomato

Chapter X

Menu Magic

It has been said that creating beautifully balanced menus is a skill and an art form. Menus need to deliver what the occasion promises—be it a simple lunch or a big cocktail celebration. The choice of dishes needs to be in harmony with the season, and they need to tell a story.

There are single-subject menus (tomatoes); special-occasion menus (birthday, anniversary or Chinese New Year); inventive themes ("American in Paris"); seasonal menus ("Last Gasp of Summer"); or time-honored Little Meals ("Breakfast in Bed," "An Afternoon Tea" or "Midnight Supper") to delight the taste buds and stimulate the imagination.

Much of menu making is intuitive and commonsensical. Good menus have a balance of flavors and contrasts of textures and temperatures. Crunch, zip, pop, crackle, slurp and pucker are the sounds that menus are made of. The rainbow is its colors. We want our mouths to water by inviting all the senses to the table: sight, sound, touch, smell and taste. We want to tickle each of our taste buds with salty, sweet, sour and bitter, all at once or one by one.

Most bewitching of all is the ability to re-create a time or a far-away place, or to evoke a mood simply by putting a few Little Meal ideas together.

The following combinations are some of my favorites. Make your own kind of magic.

Caribbean Winter

Goombay Cocktails

Lobster & Banana Calypso

Goombay Chicken & Baked
Pineapple

Candied Ginger Cake, Vanilla
Ice Cream

New Year's Eve

Shrimp Cocktail "On the Rocks"

Cake of Steak Tartare "Iced" with
Black Caviar

Pan-Seared Foie Gras, Sun-Dried
Cranberry Sauce

Déjeuner sur l'Herbe

Couscous Chicken with Orange &
Almonds, Yogurt Drizzle

Pearl Barley & Tuna Niçoise

Tian of Eggplant & Tomato, Goat
Cheese Crouton

Lunch in Tuscany

Leaning Tower of Mozzarella

Carpaccio Gold

Pasta Rustica

Sausage, Pepper & Olive Ragout

My Gypsy Mother

Beet & Fennel Borscht, Boiled Potato

Cabbage & Noodles

Palacsintas with Apricot Jam

Oriental Accents

Pork Honey Buns, Chinese-style

Orange-Ginger Lamb Riblets

"Mange-tout" Sesame Noodles

Ginger Tea

Four O'Clock

Iced Fruit Soup

A Little Afternoon Tea

Candied Ginger Cake, Vanilla Ice
Cream

Tex-Mex Fest

King Crab, Grapefruit & Avocado
Salad, Chile-Lime Dressing

Seafood Quesadilla, Triple-Decker

Espresso Bean Chili

TV Dinner

Do-It-Yourself Guacamole Kit

"Couch Potatoes"

Sticky Pears, Maple-Nut Sauce

Jazz Brunch

Gazpacho Mary with Cheese Toast

Fried Green Tomatoes, Rosemary Mayonnaise

New Orleans Shrimp & Chicken Creole, Cornbread Toast

South of the Border

Grilled Chorizos, Jicama-Orange Salad

Mexican Corn & Rice Salad, Jumbo Shrimp

Olé *Mole* in Flour Tortillas

Far East Flavors

Curried Ginger Chicken, Poppadum Crisp

Jade Rice with Shrimp & Scallops

Spicy Thai Chicken with Red Peppers & Peanuts

Dining Light

Succotash Chowder

Chardonnay Chicken & Grapes on Minted Rice

99-Calorie Crème Caramel

Picnic in Provence

Pousse Rapière

St. Tropez Tart

Scallops Provençale on Olive Toast

Steak Piperade

Ladies Who Lunch

White Wine

Poached Salmon with Cucumber-Mint Frappé

Napoleon of Gorgonzola, Pears & Walnuts

The Mediterranean Table

Warm Walnut Hummus, Chilled Vegetable Salad

Cumin Chicken on Pita Bread Salad

Seared Salmon on a Moroccan Salad

Valentine's Day
(or A Study of Tomatoes)

Cherry Tomato Boboli

Cupid's Meatloaf, Tomato Glaze & Onion Arrows

Sweet Baked Tomato

Elegant but Cheap

Baked Goat Cheese with Lima Beans & Bacon

The $2 Little Meal

Watermelon & Bitter Chocolate Salad

Restorative Little Meal

(Comfort Food)

Pastina in Garlic Broth

Cabbage & Noodles

99-Calorie Crème Caramel

Dine, Dance, Romance!

Seviche, Straight Up, with a Twist

Silver-Dollar Crabcakes, Tomato-Corn Relish

Filet Mignonettes, Celery Sticks & Blue Cheese Dressing

Little Meal for a Mayor

(or Ed Koch's Favorites)

Chicken Soup Live! (with Regis & Kathie Lee)

Caesar Salad with Roasted Red Pepper, Prosciutto Breadsticks

Ultralight Chocolate Cake

Alphabetical Recipe List

Index

About the Author

As culinary director of the Joseph Baum & Michael Whiteman Company, ROZANNE GOLD is one of New York's most influential food consultants and has created menus for the legendary Rainbow Room, Hudson River Club and restaurants world-wide. At the age of twenty-three she was first chef to New York's Mayor Ed Koch, then became the youngest female executive chef in the country for Lord & Taylor. As a food-trends expert, Ms. Gold appears regularly on national television. She is past president of Les Dames d'Escoffier, New York, and lives in Park Slope, Brooklyn, with her husband, Michael Whiteman.